TAKING UP YOUR
CROSS

TAKING UP YOUR
CROSS

TRICIA MCCARY RHODES

BETHANY HOUSE PUBLISHERS
MINNEAPOLIS, MINNESOTA 55438

Published by Bethany House Publishers
A Ministry of Bethany Fellowship International
11400 Hampshire Avenue South
Minneapolis, Minnesota 55438
www.bethanyhouse.com

Printed in the United States of America by
Bethany Press International, Minneapolis, Minnesota 55438

Library of Congress Cataloging-in-Publication Data

Rhodes, Tricia McCary.
    Taking up your cross : the incredible gain of the crucified life / by Tricia
McCary Rhodes.
      p. cm.
    ISBN 0–7642–2206–6
    1. Christian life. I. Title.
BV4501.2 .R487   2000   99–050580
248.4—dc21   CIP

To my son Champ,
whose fight for God-centeredness in all things
has transformed my thinking
and changed my life.

TRICIA McCARY RHODES is an author and speaker, a pastor's wife, and mother of two from San Diego, California. Her writings flow from twenty-five years of full-time ministry and a longing to glorify God by finding her greatest joy in Him.

If you are interested in knowing more about Tricia's ministry, you can reach her at:

New Hope Church
10330 Carmel Mountain Road
San Diego, CA 92129

(858) 538–0888, ext. 111

or e-mail at tpraynow@aol.com

ACKNOWLEDGMENTS

Mother Teresa often said she saw herself as just a stub of a pencil that God chose to pick up and write with as He pleased. I am eternally grateful for the many people whom God has *picked up* and used to write on the pages of my own life. Though the list is endless, some have made such a profound impact that I am compelled to glorify God by mentioning them.

I rejoice in having learned from saints of ages past: spiritual intimacy from Madame Jeanne Guyon, the depths of grace from Thomas à Kempis, unfettered devotion from Francois Fenelon, joy-filled obedience from Augustine, wild abandonment from Francis of Assisi, the simplicity of prayer from Teresa of Avila, the treasures of spiritual darkness from John of the Cross, and the wonder of a God-intoxicated mind from Jonathan Edwards.

Many authors of my own generation have touched my life as well through their books: A. W. Tozer, a prophet before his time, showed me a calling so lofty I am still struck with awe. Dick Eastman first opened my eyes to the inner prayer journey, and Richard Foster and Brennan Manning have been like big brothers, guiding, drawing, and continually encouraging me that there is always more in this wonderful journey with Christ.

In recent years one author has profoundly impacted not only my life but also that of my family and our church. I do not believe it is an exaggeration to say that he may be a modern-day Martin Luther to duty-driven evangelicals. His name is John Piper. I glorify God continually for the doors of freedom and joy his writings have opened to me, as he holds high the banner of God's supremacy against a weak and insipid man-centered gospel.

There are others, lesser known, but as powerfully used in my life: my sons, Champ and Jonathan, who daily cheer me on in the walk God has ordained for me; my husband, Joe, whose gentle grace has shown me a much better way for over twenty-five years; my mom, my sisters, and others of my family who season my life often with tasty nuggets of spiritual fare; and my editor, Steve Laube, who challenges and yet frees me to write only the things God speaks. I thank God for all of you.

There is one group without whom this book could not have been written. They are prayer warriors, diligent sisters and brothers who interceded often, responding in haste to my every cry for help (and there were many). Thank you, dear ones—may you enjoy the eternal reward of your labor of joy and love.

Most important, to the living God, who is passionate about His own glory and loves me enough to use me in spite of myself (a reality I never get accustomed to)—with all that is within me I offer a simple prayer of thanksgiving. You made my joy to overflow as you led me through the journey of writing this book. I love you, my precious Redeemer. May you ever be praised, lifted high, and glorified as you so deserve.

CONTENTS

LETTER TO THE READER

Dearest Reader,

A year and a half ago God impressed upon my heart a call to write about what it means to take up our cross. Having been deeply and profoundly changed by my own encounter with the crucified Christ, this seemed a natural follow-up for myself and for those who had journeyed to the Cross through my writing.[1]

I was unprepared for what happened next. Almost immediately I entered a sort of spiritual depression. Because the Lord long ago convicted me that I must not write something I had not experienced, I felt certain that the next several months were going to be gruesome as I sought to take up my own cross and die to self. The burden of the call became like a weight on my shoulders, and I felt an almost continual ache in the pit of my stomach. This went on for days, to the extent that when I ran into a friend I'd not seen in several months, she asked if a tragedy had taken place. Everyone I talked to commiserated that God had called me to write something so *deep* and *difficult*.

Then one morning in prayer, God spoke gently to my heart these thoughts: *Tricia, you've got it all wrong, and much of my church has it all wrong. Dying to self is not about what you give up but about what you gain—it's all about gain.* Immediately the load lifted and a sense of joy flooded my entire being. Over the next several days God impressed me with simple words—words like "contentment" and "quietness" and "gentleness" and "humility"—saying that these are the things that become ours as we take up our cross.

Writing this book has been a difficult yet glorious journey. It has been difficult to let God change my thinking, radically altering some deep-seated beliefs about what it means to follow Him. It has been glorious to experience His grace in a profound and freeing new way, filling me with unspeakable joy. I am not the same person I was, and the story of what happened to me is filtered throughout the pages you are about to read.

If I were to summarize the driving theme of what I've learned, it would be this: All sin is simply desire gone awry, and, therefore, dying to self is about learning to fling aside a nature that can never find God, that can never have its deepest needs met, that hangs on only to run here and there, frantic for a fulfillment that will never come.

From the materialistic man to the self-absorbed teenager, the anorexic to the homosexual, the alcoholic to the driven businesswoman, the blatant idolater to the bored believer, desire gone awry wreaks nothing but a devastating destruction from which God longs to rescue us.

The incredible truth is that our precious Lord has already done everything necessary to enable us to live in the joy of the crucified life. The old self with its lusts of deceit is on a continual road to corruption. For now, at times, it may seem like a bloated balloon, but in reality it is slowly losing air and one day will crumple lifeless before our very eyes. Our new self is already complete—in the likeness of God it *has been* created in righteousness and holiness of truth (Ephesians 4:22–24). All that is left for us to do is to stretch out our arms to the living God, letting Him wrap us in our beautiful new robes. When this happens, every desire we've ever known will finally be met in the glory of the One who died for us.

Thus if you picked up this book looking for hard-hitting admonitions on a life of chastity and denial, you will not find it, but perhaps you'll discover something better. If you're hoping for some formula, some trick that will make dying to self a manageable component of your spiritual walk, you might be disappointed, but, then again, you just might discover something more profoundly practical.

I am convinced that our greatest need is not for more information or for greater diligence or discipline, but for a fresh revelation of the Savior, who ever lives to fill our lives with abundance and joy. Once we see Him, once we get even a glimpse of what He offers, we will be relieved to throw aside the rags of self that have kept us from experiencing our very birthright as believers.

I pray with everything within me that God will make this your experience as you take up your cross and follow the blessed and precious Lover of our souls.

In His wondrous love,
Tricia McCary Rhodes

P.S. For those of you who have journeyed with God through my other two books, you will find this one a little different. It does not have daily devotional exercises because I felt that this type of teaching is best assimilated through extended times with God. Thus I have provided a mini-retreat at the end of each chapter to allow you to experience God in His way for you. Please take the time to do these. I am convinced the greatest impact will be seen as God manifests himself to you personally. Without that, all my words are only words, lacking any power to change or enrich you.

Note

1. See Tricia McCary Rhodes, *Contemplating the Cross* (Minneapolis: Bethany House Publishers, 1998).

CHAPTER ONE
HOLINESS

The unfathomable mystery of God is that God is a Lover who wants to be loved. The One who created us is waiting for our response to the love that gave us our being. God not only says, "You are my beloved." God also asks, "Do you love me?" and offers countless chances to say yes.[1]

Henri Nouwen

As a child, I remember crawling under my mahogany bunk bed, face pressed to the cool dark wall, cherishing the quiet space where dreams came to life and anything seemed possible. Later, through the wonder of books, I often lost myself in the pages of someone else's journey. I cried for the distant dreams of lovers long ago and pondered the conundrums of life across some great divide in another time. Something within me has always felt a bit ill-placed in this world—as if I've wandered into a stranger's home unawares.

Perhaps you've experienced this odd phenomenon as well. I know I'm not alone. I've seen wonder glistening in my young son's eyes as he wields his light saber against extraterrestrial foes. I've heard the wistful tone in my older son's voice as he tries to explain the compelling power of the ocean over his soul after a day of surfing. I see it on faces in unlikely sound bites of life, this inner yearning that has neither form nor substance to meld with reality. Mothers sigh in grocery checkout lines, assaulted by the headlines of the day, and families move en masse to hidden hollows in the Pacific Northwest looking for some critical but elusive piece of life's puzzle.

The writers of an intriguing book called *The Sacred Romance* contend that these yearnings are evidence of the wooing of God himself—the eternal Lover of our souls. They write, "Someone or something has romanced us from the beginning with creek-side singers and pastel sunsets, with the austere majesty of snowcapped mountains and the poignant flames of autumn colors telling us of something—or someone—leaving with a promise to return."[2]

The authors go on to suggest that God has placed within us a need for wonder and mystery that may translate into a man's desire for adventure and a woman's for intimacy. Perhaps they are right. From the Lone Ranger of my husband's childhood to the Luke Skywalker of my son's, what boy has not dreamed of heroes bigger than life who could win the day? From Sleeping Beauty to Princess Jasmine, what girl has not fantasized of a Prince Charming or an Aladdin who could capture her heart and carry her to a place where life was glorious and miracles commonplace?

Can this really be? Have the unspoken yearnings of our soul been put there to draw us to the living God, a lover who dances into our dreams and schemes with the promise of fulfillment? Is He flirting with us when He sprays the sky with a multihued sunset or shatters the silence with frightening roars of thunderclap? Does He watch our wonder and wait to see if we're impressed as He leaps in the shadows for joy over His works? If so, what are we to do? How are we to respond to such magnificent exhibitions? And what might this have to do with holiness?

The answer to these questions holds mystery and wonder, adventure and intimacy. In a drama transcending time and space, the lead player is the great I AM, who has always been and always will be. In His manifold perfection as God, He lacks nothing. Yet, before the foundation of this world, He chose a people to be His own, who would belong to Him and be called by His Name—a people for whom He would be the love of their life and hope for their future.

Those who hear and respond to His call are *chosen of God, holy and beloved* (Colossians 3:12), saved with a holy calling for the Lord God's purposes (2 Timothy 1:9). At salvation He betroths himself to us, promising that He will come again, riding on a white horse, eyes flaming with fire and a sword in His hand to redeem His bride (Revelation 19:11–17).

Imagine—we will one day see Him face-to-face—this One who has romanced and wooed us and for whom we've ached with love. The reality that "I am my beloved's, and his desire is for me" (Song of Solomon 7:10) can only captivate us, infusing our waking moments with amazement. We long to be holy, set apart for our Bridegroom, dressed in readiness day in and day out, the flame of our hearts burning with passionate adoration.

Nothing can give vision and purpose to our life on earth like the truth that we are a holy people, chosen and set apart to be Christ's bride. In awe, we anticipate the moment our eternal Lover will take us home to be wed, "holy and blameless, having no spot or wrinkle or any such thing" (Ephesians 5:27).

HOLINESS

*Embracing my sacred destiny as one chosen by Christ,
the Lover of my soul.*

Foundations for Holiness

The concept of holiness is so significant that it is referenced over six hundred times in Scripture. Perhaps some of the most powerful words written were those given by Moses to the Israelites some fourteen times and later quoted by Peter to the New Testament church: *Be holy, for I am holy.*

What does this really mean? What is holiness from a practical perspective, and how can we obey such a weighty decree? A deeper understanding of the following three truths is helpful: God is holy; God has chosen us to be His own; God is a jealous lover.

God Is Holy

Fresh fallen snow . . . a newborn babe . . . a virgin bride . . . a white-hot flame. These images, which the word "holy" elicits, all have one thing in common—they are untainted, without blemish. Yet these are only temporary conditions. The purity of each cannot last. Rain turns snow to mud, and flames burn out.

But there is One whose very essence is a radiant purity that can never fade. He is the Lord. Every attempt we make to characterize His holiness falls short. He is not just purer than the purest thing we can think of, but He is inherently pure and thus beyond understanding. He transcends us in every way, making His holiness incomprehensible to our finite minds. We have nothing with which to compare it. " 'To whom then will you liken me that I would be his equal?' says the Holy One" (Isaiah 40:25). And we can only answer: "There is no one holy like the Lord, indeed, there is no one besides you" (1 Samuel 2:2).

Holy is the prefix to God's name more than any other attribute in Scripture, for it is the foundation of His character. It makes everything about Him faultless and complete and unlike us. His goodness isn't like ours, rising and falling on the strength of emotion—it is *holy goodness*—always good, perfectly good. His mercies endure forever because they are *holy* mercies. His greatness is unsurpassable for it is *holy* greatness.

In the heavenlies, one word reverberates in triple ovations around the throne: "Holy, holy, holy" (Isaiah 6:3; Revelation 4:8). To see even a twinkling of God's holiness would likely stun us into silence as it did the prophets Habakkuk and Zechariah. Unless God reveals it to us, our understanding of

His holiness will never be more than a miniscule thread in an infinite tapestry of knowledge.

One physicist who spends his waking hours considering the cosmos speaks of the immensity of infinity and the mystery of time and space with all its complexities. He suggests that more than most he has a heightened appreciation for what he calls the "magnitude of God's domain." Yet he writes, "But what overrides all of this is the pure heaviness (for lack of a better term) of *the holiness of the Lord Almighty* . . . once one is aware of the magnitude of this, all else becomes trite, quite frankly . . . awesome, awesome holiness."[3]

God's holiness sets Him apart from everything and everyone, sealing His sovereign supremacy unto infinity. "Who will not fear, O Lord, and glorify Your name? For You alone are holy; for all the nations will come and worship before You, for Your righteous acts have been revealed" (Revelation 15:4). The Lord is holy, and when we grasp this at all, undone and sobered at our own sinful state, we will fall at His feet in worship.

God Has Chosen Us to Be His Own

When God commands us to *be holy as He is holy*, He is not saying we will ever be the essence of holiness, for then He would cease to be God. His holiness is what makes Him the transcendent Other. But in this command, He discloses one of the most profound mysteries in the universe. Elohim, the one supreme God, calls out a people to be His own, a people on whom He will have mercy and for whom He will accept the payment of His Son's death for the wrath He feels at their sin.

" 'They will be mine,' says the Lord of hosts, 'on the day that I prepare My own possession, and I will spare them as a man spares his own son who serves him' " (Malachi 3:17). Though we may endlessly debate the issue of free will versus predestination, we who have come to know the living God through His Son must live in utter astonishment that He would choose anyone at all.

Why would a self-contained and gloriously independent God call out a people to be His own? Scripture makes it clear: "But you are a chosen race, a royal priesthood, a holy nation, a people for God's own possession, so that you may proclaim the excellencies of Him who has called you out of darkness into His marvelous light" (1 Peter 2:9). God wants to make us into what C. S. Lewis calls "a dazzling, radiant, immortal creature, pulsating all through with such energy and joy and wisdom and love as we cannot now imagine, a bright stainless mirror that reflects back to God perfectly (though of course, on a smaller scale) His own boundless power and delight and goodness."[4]

Cities upon a hill, God sets our hearts aflame that we might cast His brilliant light across the expanse of a darkened globe and back to His own heart. Like beautiful jewels adorning His attire, He desires that we cling to Him so that we might be a "people for renown, for praise, and for glory" (Jeremiah 13:11). This is why He sets us apart. This is what it means to be holy.

God Is a Jealous Lover

When God chooses us to be His own, He gives us nothing less than himself. Out of His holy perfection, He delights in sharing all that He is. Ultimately He knows this will lead to His glory, for as He gives, we come to know Him intimately, deep adoration flooding our souls. He calls out, "I will betroth you to me forever; yes, I will betroth you to me in righteousness and in justice, in lovingkindness and in compassion, and I will betroth you to me in faithfulness. Then you will know the Lord" (Hosea 2:19–20).

When we break our engagement covenant with God and fall into sin, two things take place. First, His name is profaned. God told the Israelites that when their sins defeated them, other nations concluded their God was weak and ineffective (Joshua 24:19). When Jesus is not the consuming passion that drives all other passions from our soul, those who watch our faith can only conclude He is not a worthy lover. This thwarts the very purpose for which He chose us: "My holy name I will make known . . . and I will not let My holy name be profaned anymore. And the nations will know that I am the Lord, the Holy One in Israel" (Ezekiel 39:7).

The second thing that happens when our faithfulness to God wanes is we are robbed of pleasure. God knows that anything that takes us from Him will destroy our joy and fulfillment in Him. This is why He told the Israelites when they went into Canaan that if they made covenants with the people there, they would become trapped by them. He warned them instead to tear down all the altars, smashing their sacred pillars and cutting down their idols, worshiping Him only, "for the Lord, whose name is Jealous, is a jealous God" (Exodus 34:12–14). God is jealous for our joy in Him and filled with wrath at anything that threatens it.

Barriers to Holiness

What keeps us from living as God's cherished possession? Why would we resist such a calling? Perhaps it has to do with the word itself. For many, holiness represents an unattainable lifestyle, conjuring up thoughts of legalistic perfectionism. It is a common mistake to translate God's desire for our souls into do's and don'ts for our days. Trading a sort of "pseudo-holiness" for the real thing, we find it easier to manage a list of behaviors than to have our hearts transformed.

But as Richard Foster notes, these "miss the point of a life hidden with God in Christ. No single standard of behavior is dictated by the word holy. All external legalisms fail to capture the heart of holy living and holy dying."[5] So why do we settle for a dry and outer form rather than true holiness?

We Don't See Ourselves As God's Treasure

Do you remember the thrill of your first love? Can you recall how you treasured him (or her), thinking of him day and night, longing to be in his presence and shower him with affection? In the same way, our Lord is enamored with us. When He takes us to be His own, He rejoices over us as a bridegroom over a bride (Isaiah 62:3–5). We are the object of His desire—a gift to the Son from the Father and a treasured one at that. "Jesus knows that the Father only gives good gifts. Yes, we are imperfect, but Christ sees us the way His grace shall ultimately create us. And what kind of gift are we? Are we a reward or, perhaps, a challenge? No. We are His bride. The glance of our eyes makes His heart beat faster" (Song of Solomon 4:9).[6]

Awe-inspiring thoughts. Yet we struggle to accept this and live in the wonder of it. Why? Paradoxically, the culprit is pride. Pride is the subtle notion that I must commend myself to God through my ability or actions. It manifests itself in pendulumlike fashion—I think I should be able to earn His adoration, or I live in fear that I never will. Both of these produce defeat.

When we try to win God's affection, it's usually through diligence, obedience, and hard work. Aren't these good things? They can be, but we have to ask ourselves why we are so diligent, so obedient. For years I labored, striving to gain what Christ had already given me out of the storehouse of His infinite love. Ever living to prove my value to Him, I didn't know how to bask in the ardor of a God who chose me not because of my spiritual prowess but simply because He loved me (Deuteronomy 7:7–8).

There are others, equally bound, who live in fear they'll never get it right, suffering from a sort of inverted pride. Their perpetual self-condemnation denies God's unconditional love and rejects the tender mercies He ever lives to pour out. A tyrant husband throwing his weight around in front of a cowering wife is a troubling prospect, and it must terribly grieve the heart of God when we view Him that way. A. W. Tozer wrote, "We do God more honor by believing what He has said about Himself and having the courage to come boldly to the throne of grace than by hiding in self-conscious humility among the trees of the garden."[7] Saddest of all, in our hiding we fail to experience the passionate embrace of our eternal Lover.

We are God's treasure through nothing we have ever done, a truth we must cling to and dwell upon. Because He is holy and perfect, we in our fallen humanity cannot warrant or earn His affection. It is not our attractiveness that compels God to choose us, but His choice of us that makes us attractive, turning us into "the stones of a crown, sparkling in His land. For what comeliness and beauty will be theirs!" (Zechariah 9:16–17). God is a lover, and the minute we become His, He drenches our souls in the glory of His adoration, making us shine back to Him like precious jewels. This is what makes us the objects of His desire. This is what makes us holy.

We Do Not Live for His Appearing

Living near a major naval base, I have often watched ships deploy for lengthy missions overseas. Newsclips of families saying good-bye at the dock are heart-wrenching. The spouses and children hold their loved ones until the very last second, dreading the days and nights of distance between them. But soon the ship leaves, the media fades away, and we forget about children without fathers or mothers, or lonely spouses. The families go on as if life were normal—eating, sleeping, going to school and work, and making important decisions.

Yet when the ship comes in, it is clear that those who were left behind have lived for this moment. Bearing homemade welcome signs, carrying balloons and flowers, and wearing shiny new clothes, they watch eagerly for the face of their beloved to disembark from the ship. When he (or she) appears, running with all his (her) might, the family flings themselves into the arms of this one for whom they've waited so long.

On the night before His death, Jesus assured His disciples that He was going to prepare a place for them, and that He would come back to bring them home with Him one day (John 14:3). The early church held onto this promise like a lifeline, even as their world fell apart and their lives were in constant danger. *Come quickly, Lord Jesus* was the cry of their heart.

Do you live with eager anticipation of our Lord's return? When God is the Lover of our soul, we long for Him in His fullness. We look at our world darkened by evil and groan for His purity to permeate it. We feel our separation from Him in painful ways. "The Bridegroom whom we love was taken away. The wedding party was broken up. It is as though the wedding march had started and we were walking down the aisle to Him, and at the last minute He disappeared."[8]

Because Jesus graciously left us His Spirit, we can exist in a world devoid of His physical presence, but every day we "groan within ourselves, waiting eagerly for our adoption as sons" (Romans 8:23). We are consumed with the realization that "eye has not seen and ear has not heard . . . all that God has prepared for those who love Him" (1 Corinthians 2:9). We live for and love His appearing, waiting for the day He will place a crown of righteousness on our head (2 Timothy 4:8).

To love His appearing is far more than a pie-in-the-sky escape from this world. Every day He comes to us—every minute He continues to woo us, dazzling us with amorous overtures. To love His appearing is to be so smitten by Jesus that we think of Him all the time. We're neither enticed by other lovers nor distracted by the busyness of life. Thoughts of Him pervade all that we do. We cry out, "Hurry, my beloved, and be like a gazelle or a young stag on the mountain of spices" (Song of Solomon 8:14).

Living in a love affair with our Lord and believing His promise to come again compels us to keep ourselves clothed and ready for Him. We want to be a pure and spotless bride and do all that we can to prepare for the great wedding supper of the Lamb. Nothing He asks of us is too hard—His commands are not burdensome (1 John 5:3), for love motivates all we do. Like Jacob, who worked fourteen years to make Rachel his own (Genesis 29:30), we say from our heart that we so adore our Beloved that the time spent waiting for Him seems like nothing.

We Take God's Jealousy Lightly

Imagine a wife coming home several days in a row, telling her husband the details of lunch dates she's been having with a wonderful new man at work. When the husband calls for an end to their relationship, she protests,

"I do everything you ask me to. I cook, clean, warm your bed, raise your children, and entertain your bosses. How could you object to this small pleasure in my life?"

Or suppose a husband blatantly flirts with other women every time he takes his wife out. When she finally calls him on it, he is surprised, telling her, "I'm just having a little fun. When have I ever cheated on you?"

No one would willingly enter such a relationship. Yet many of us treat our union with God that way. We do what we're supposed to do. We go to church, read our Bible, pray, witness, and may even teach a Sunday school class. We've fulfilled our vows and don't understand why God should care about things like the movies we see, the money we spend, the jokes we tell, or the recreations we pursue.

But the great I AM has paid dearly with the blood of His only Son to make us His own. He's given us His Holy Spirit as a pledge of betrothal, guaranteeing His loyalty (1 Corinthians 6:19–20). Thus He is intimately mindful of our affections, becoming "a consuming fire, a jealous God" (Deuteronomy 4:24) when we are seduced by other lovers, no matter how inconsequential they may seem.

When the clothes we wear or the career we pursue or the child we adore or the money we invest elicits greater pleasure than the presence of our Divine Lover, then He has been replaced as the object of our soul's affection. James called this spiritual adultery, making the sober proclamation that to be friends of this world means to be an enemy of God (James 4:4). This affects everything in our lives. God warned the Israelites that though they called Him father and friend, their involvement with foreign gods and cultures was an adultery that polluted the entire land (Jeremiah 3:1–2).

Any spouse whose marriage partner has been unfaithful knows the devastation it wreaks. But oh how much greater the agony when that same spouse does not take his (or her) actions seriously, behaving as if they aren't all that important. The relationship can only suffer irreparable damage. In the same way, when we take God's jealousy over our betrayals lightly, we grieve His Holy Spirit by whom we were sealed for the day of redemption (Ephesians 4:30). If we truly felt the pain we inflict on God through our seemingly innocuous infidelities, we would run to Him in repentance and remorse. To be indifferent is to be unholy.

What We Must Do

Years ago at dinner with my parents and some friends, the conversation turned to a popular movie some of us had seen. Someone mentioned the sexual content, and we all agreed it could have been omitted but didn't ruin the movie. My father shook his head, saying, "I think it's wrong, and we shouldn't be going to those."

Embarrassed for those who'd seen it, I quickly responded, "Oh, Dad, it wasn't that bad, and besides, things have changed."

An abrupt silence ensued, my words hanging in the air until Mom quickly offered everyone dessert. When my father died the next year, the memory of that conversation was my only regret. I loved my father dearly. We'd been extremely close and never had angry words. But in that one interaction, I'd dishonored him and never taken the time to say I was sorry. I grieved not only that I'd spoken so quickly but also that I hadn't valued what my father valued in life. Confessing it to the Lord, I received forgiveness, wishing Dad were there to talk with.

Years later this memory flashed before my mind as I sought God's face in prayer one morning. Waiting quietly on Him, I heard with painful conviction: "Tricia, you understood then what it meant to dishonor your father's heart by not valuing what he valued, but have you ever grasped how you grieve my heart in the same way?"

Tears flowing, I admitted insensitivity to God's feelings about the sin in my life. Though my behavior was impeccable by many people's standards, God wanted me to know that holiness was a heart condition. It meant feeling what He felt, loving what He loved, and caring deeply about the things He cared about, no matter how insignificant they might seem to me at the time.

Sanctification From the Heart

In the first chapter of his letter to the scattered and persecuted church, Peter, quoting from the Torah, admonishes them to be holy. For the next two chapters, he addresses various relationships—servant and master, husband and wife, citizen and government—detailing proper Christian attitudes and responses. He ends the exhortation with these words: "But sanctify Christ as Lord in your hearts" (1 Peter 3:15). Peter knew that holy behavior could only come from a holy heart.

To be sanctified is to have a holy heart, one that watches carefully to see God's agenda. It takes nothing lightly, clinging to every word, running to obey. A holy heart wants to please the Holy One, not out of a need for approval, but out of honor and love.

Moses experienced the raw agony of unholiness—of not following from the heart. Over and over God had spoken through him to the Israelites: "Be holy, for I am holy." When Moses tired of the people's complaints about the lack of water, he took his frustrations to God, who gave him very specific instructions to speak to a rock, promising water would burst forth.

Moses went from that encounter still consumed with his own agenda of anger toward the people's rejection of his leadership. Instead of speaking to the rock, he hit it twice. And though God in His mercy let the water pour out, He took great issue with Moses for his disobedience. "Because you have not believed Me, to treat Me as holy in the sight of the sons of Israel, therefore you shall not bring this assembly into the land which I have given them" (Numbers 20:12). Moses' failure to connect heart to heart with God's true purpose was an unholy response.

Sanctification produces inner purity that handles every word God speaks with tender care. Though it is a process of growth and maturity, we must pursue it wholeheartedly. Every sin we harbor is an assault on the holiness of God. When we fail to treat Him as holy, we fail to sanctify Him as Lord in our hearts, an offense so serious Moses lost the blessing of leading God's people into the Promised Land.

The Gift of Holiness

Peter admonished the early church to be holy in *all* their behavior, emphasizing God's holiness as their standard (1 Peter 1:15). For centuries people have struggled with this, often vacillating between guilty frustration and legalistic pride. It seems an impossible task, and it is. Paul explains that God "saved us, and called us with a holy calling, not according to our works, but according to His own purpose and grace which was granted us in Christ Jesus from all eternity" (2 Timothy 1:9).

Holiness is a gift of grace and can never be achieved through human effort. At conversion, God's Holy Spirit enters our spirit creating a new self whose very nature is full of "righteousness and holiness of the truth" (Ephesians 4:24). What incredible possibilities this opens to our soul. Through no merit of our own, the Father draws our heart to himself, the blood of His Son separates us from an unholy world, and the Spirit puts to death our old self so that we can walk in newness of life.

This "sanctifying work of the Spirit" (1 Peter 1:2) is what enables us to live holy lives. In our own flesh we can never conjure up affection toward our Beloved, nor can we hope to attain the high standard of perfection He is worthy of. What peace in knowing the Holy Spirit of the living God began this good work in us and will perfect it until the day we see Jesus face-to-face (Philippians 1:6). Our part is to simply take up our cross by calling upon the Holy Spirit within to deliver us from unholy thoughts or behavior that might grieve our beloved Savior.

Romance Versus Duty

My first love was a high school sweetheart to whom I pledged my undying devotion. Through our teen years we spent as much time as possible together and went away to college determined to marry as soon as we could afford it. Though I don't know when things fell apart, I do remember the moment I realized we were in trouble. One Friday as we talked about what to do with the long evening ahead, he said he was tired and really just wanted to go to his room and do nothing. Like a jolt to my senses, the reality that he did not want to be with me for the first time I could ever remember produced overwhelming sadness.

Several weeks later the relationship limped to an end as I admitted to myself that somewhere along the way he'd stopped loving me. And though we'd gone through the motions for months, I finally understood that for him, staying with me had become an obligation, a duty from which he didn't know how to extricate himself. The day I returned the engagement ring, though heartbroken, I was also relieved, for the romantic role he'd continued to act out had become a burden I could no longer bear.

God expressed a similar weariness one day to His beloved—the nation of Israel. They were dutifully doing all the things they thought they should to maintain their relationship with Him. Faithfully they executed a multitude of offerings, feasts, and solemn assemblies, assuming this would be enough to satisfy God. Instead He recoiled, telling them they didn't understand who He really was. Spent with grief, He cried:

> An ox knows its owner, and a donkey its master's manger, but Israel does not know, My people do not understand. . . . They have abandoned the Lord, they have despised the Holy One of Israel, they have turned away from Him . . . "What are your multiplied sacrifices to me?" says the Lord. "I have had enough . . . Bring your worthless offerings no longer . . . I hate your new moon festivals and your appointed feasts, they have become a burden to Me; I am weary of bearing them" (Isaiah 1:1–14, selected).

God is not interested in the driven works of a dutiful spouse but instead longs for the romantic response of a delighted lover.

One pastor I know often challenges his congregation with two questions. First, "Are you spending time in God's presence daily?" And second, "Is it duty, or is it romance?" Faithfulness to God as the Lover of our souls can never be fulfilled out of duty. If we try, we will miss the joy and God will take no pleasure in the endless list of works we do in His name. How we demean the passionate love of our Lord when we serve Him out of obligation instead of a heart that pines for His presence.

An Astounding Invitation

I remember the days when grocery stores first started opening on Sundays. It was quite a dilemma for our Southern Baptist family. We'd always followed God's command to remember the Sabbath and keep it holy, which meant going to church twice, taking an afternoon nap, and never frequenting any establishment that opened their doors. But slowly the stigma faded, and like everyone else we began to go to the store when we needed something.

I often wondered what it really meant to keep the Sabbath holy after that. As the years went on, Sundays bore a striking resemblance to the rest of the week, except instead of going to work, we went to church. Recently as I studied God's holiness I was taken aback by the following passage: "If because of the sabbath, you turn your foot from doing your own pleasure on My holy day, and call the sabbath a delight, the holy day of the Lord honorable, and honor it, desisting from your own ways, from seeking your own pleasure, and speaking your own word, then you will take delight in the Lord" (Isaiah 58:13–14a).

God never intended the Sabbath to be a day of holy rules and regulations. His desire was for His people to take one day each week to discard all other affections, set aside every distraction, and honor Him by spending the entire day delighting in His presence. What He promised if they would do this was absolutely astounding: "I will make you ride on the heights of the earth; and I will feed you with the heritage of Jacob your father, for the mouth of the Lord has spoken" (v. 14b).

The author of Hebrews tells us that as partakers of the new covenant, our entire life is to be a sabbath rest. Every day of every week, every moment of every hour we are to rest from the burden of duty-driven religion and enter the delight of loving God.

The mouth of the Lord has spoken—can you hear His holy voice? Your deepest yearnings for adventure, for intimacy, for mystery, and for wonder that transcends this temporal existence can be fulfilled even now! Riding with Yahweh on the heights of the earth, feeding from the hand of our precious Redeemer Jesus Christ—these are the rewards of a holy life. As one old saint said, "Beyond this, we cannot go in this world; but short of this we ought never to rest."[9]

But oh, wondrous thought—this is only the engagement. One day our Bridegroom will come to take us as His own, consummating eternally the love affair He initiated with our souls before the foundation of the earth. Glorious, glorious promise. Don your holy garments! Make yourself ready for the wedding feast of the Lamb. Live in eager anticipation of that day when the trumpet will sound, the dead will be raised, and we will be changed.

Listen . . . approaching hoofbeats . . . can you hear them even now? "Behold, the Bridegroom! Come out to meet Him" (Matthew 25:6). May the sound of these words resound continually in our ears, filling our holy hearts with indefatigable joy.

❧　❧

TAKING UP OUR CROSS—
What We Gain and What We Lose

Holiness requires we take up our cross against anything and everything that interferes with passionate intimacy with Christ. As we do, we experience depths of love we could never have dreamed possible. Finally, we understand who we are because we have grasped Whose we are.

Gain Identity

"For you are a holy people to the Lord your God, and the Lord has chosen you to be a people for His own possession out of all the peoples who are on the face of the earth" (Deuteronomy 14:2).

Lose Shame

"Fear not, for you will not be put to shame; and do not feel humiliated, for you will not be disgraced; but you will forget the shame of your youth, and the reproach of your widowhood you will remember no more" (Isaiah 54:4).

Nothing is more tiring than the insecurity (sometimes masked as arrogance) that requires us to impress everyone at all times, including God himself. There is a freedom that comes in letting go, recognizing our own neediness, resting in our inadequacy. Often through tears, we discover the precious presence of our beloved Lord.

Gain Contrition

"For thus says the high and exalted One who lives forever, whose name is Holy, 'I dwell on a high and holy place, and also with the contrite and lowly of spirit in order to revive the spirit of the lowly and to revive the heart of the contrite'" (Isaiah 57:15).

Lose Insecurity/Arrogance

"There is no one holy like the Lord, indeed, there is no one besides you, nor is there any rock like our God. Boast no more so very proudly, do not let arrogance come out of your mouth; for the Lord is a God of knowledge, and with Him actions are weighed" (1 Samuel 2:2–3).

God loves to work wonders on behalf of His chosen people when their hearts are tuned to glorify Him. Whatever our struggles may be, however small or great, being holy—consecrated to the Lord—guarantees spiritual victory and great power against the Evil One. To refuse to turn from sin is to invite spiritual defeat, robbing us of our holy calling.

Gain Spiritual Victory

"Then Joshua said to the people, 'Consecrate yourselves, for tomorrow the Lord will do wonders among you' " (Joshua 3:5).

"For the Mighty One has done great things for me; and holy is His name" (Luke 1:49).

Lose Spiritual Defeat

"Rise up! Consecrate the people and say, 'Consecrate yourselves for tomorrow, for thus the Lord, the God of Israel, has said, "There are things under the ban in your midst, O Israel. You cannot stand before your enemies until you have removed the things under the ban from your midst" ' " (Joshua 7:13).

When Christ died for us, He cleansed us completely, setting us apart by clothing us in His righteousness. Yet every day the world beckons us to shed our holy garments and dance in the streets of perversion, impurity, immorality, and utter depravity. Though we have been sanctified, we must also continually *be sanctified* by setting our hearts toward our only True Love. When He is our partner in the dance of life, guilt flees as we experience moral strength and purity of soul.

Gain Sacred Calling

"For God has not called us for the purpose of impurity, but in sanctification" (1 Thessalonians 4:7).

"But by His doing you are in Christ Jesus, who became to us wisdom from God, and righteousness and sanctification, and redemption" (1 Corinthians 1:30).

Lose Impurity/Immorality

"For this is the will of God, your sanctification; that is that you abstain from sexual immorality; that each of you know how to possess his own vessel in sanctification and honor, not in lustful passion, like the Gentiles who do not know God" (1 Thessalonians 4:3–4).

God is deeply grieved when we fail to live holy lives. Through unbelief, we shun our Lover who has given everything to make us His own. How our hearts should break at the thought. On the other hand, when we are faithful to Him, our love is like a pleasant aroma wafting to His throne. What a joy to experience the pleasure of the Holy One in our lives.

Gain God's Pleasure

"As a soothing aroma I will accept you when I bring you out from the peoples and gather you from the lands where you are scattered; and I will prove Myself holy among you in the sight of the nations" (Ezekiel 20:41).

Lose God's Grief

"How often they rebelled against Him in the wilderness and grieved Him in the desert! Again and again they tempted God, and pained the Holy One of Israel. They did not remember His power, the day when He redeemed them from the adversary" (Psalm 78:40–42).

Oh, the wonder of being God's chosen and holy ones, called by His name. Surely we lose nothing by dying to the shame, insecurity, arrogance, defeat, and impurity that has broken the very heart of a holy God. We have everything to gain—a new identity, a contrite heart, victorious life, purity of deeds, and above all an outpouring of God's pleasure.

Holy people are so rare in this day and yet so desperately needed to bring hope to a darkened world. When we encounter one who has given herself (or himself) without abandon to our Holy God, she is "a warm hearth, a shelter that invites us to come in from the cold. Even though we sense an underlying strength that tells us sin and manipulation are not acceptable in [this person's] presence—and this can be somewhat fearful—we still find ourselves drawn [to her or him]."[10] Let us take up our cross in holiness.

PRACTICING HOLINESS—
A Mini-Retreat

Because we tend to think of holiness as the things we *do* instead of who we *are*, we can easily miss God's deeper purpose in calling us to it. Jesus said the evil we think or do comes from our heart (Matthew 15:18–19), and that is where we must begin in our quest for holiness. As you spend this extended time in God's presence, seek to let go of old misconceptions and hear His heart for you this day.

Preparing Your Heart

Take a few minutes to become still before the Lord. Thank Him for His presence, both within your soul and without. Write a short love letter welcoming Him to this time of intimacy after quietly contemplating these verses from the bride in The Song of Solomon. (Many scholars believe the bride in this book is analogous to the church, and the beloved is Christ.)

Like an apple tree among the trees of the forest, so is my beloved among the young men. In his shade I took great delight and sat down, and his fruit was sweet to my taste.

He has brought me to his banquet hall, and his banner over me is love.

Listen! My beloved! Behold, he is coming, climbing on the mountains, leaping on the hills!

My beloved is like a gazelle or a young stag. Behold, he is standing behind our wall, He is looking through the windows, He is peering through the lattice.

O my dove, in the clefts of the rock, in the secret place of the steep pathway, let me see your form, let me hear your voice; for your voice is sweet, and your form is lovely.

My beloved is mine, and I am his; He pastures his flock among the lilies. (Song of Solomon 2:3–4, 8–9, 14, 16)

Read 1 Chronicles 16:8–12, 25–36 as an offering of praise to God. Pause occasionally to consider the truth you read, experiencing the joy of it.

Meditate for a few minutes on verses 30–33. Imagine what it will be like when our Lord comes. Picture that moment when all of creation will cry out in celebration. Offer words of praise and thanksgiving.

Contemplating His Presence

When we consider the grandeur of the great and awesome Lord of the universe, we can't help but feel small and perhaps of little value in contrast. Yet with all the billions of people that have populated this universe, God's infinite nature enables Him to know every one of us intimately, to love us in very personal ways, delighting in what He has created us to be. It is truly a mystery that frail humans occupy such a tender place in the heart of God.

Oh, how His love transforms our very existence. What freedom we find in knowing that just as our righteous deeds don't increase God's love, neither does our sinfulness cause it to shrivel up. Philip Yancey notes that God's grace means He already loves us as much as an infinite God possibly can. Nothing we do will make Him love us more and nothing we do will make Him love us less.[11] He loves. Some of the most amazing words of Scripture are the romantic and reassuring words our Beloved speaks to us. We can be changed as we soak them in, experiencing the wonder of unconditional love.

Read Revelation 2:17 and 19:5–16 and Isaiah 62:2–5 in preparation for this time with the Lord. When you are finished, read the following visualization a couple of times, then contemplate the experience, listening for His personal word to you as you delight in the presence of your Eternal Lover.

It has been a very ordinary night, not unlike all the others, but you awake with a start and know that everything has changed. Like Alice with her looking glass, you have fallen into a whole new existence—a place unlike anything you've seen before. In the twinkling of an eye, you've entered eternity's gates and it takes your breath away.

All around you nature unleashes its awesome power. Lightning flashes, thunder peals, and a brilliant rainbow surrounds what appears to be the centerpiece of all—a glorious throne. Voices fill the air with singing—increasing in volume to a monumental roar, then settling into soft, gentle harmony. You look around at the vast sea of faces—people of every age, nationality, and language imaginable flood your vision for as far as you can see. Many wave palm branches, and the breeze of their worship wafts over your being like a peaceful sonnet.

Noticing their brilliant and beautiful robes, you glance down self-consciously, only to find that you, too, have been clothed with a garment so pure it seems to radiate light. All of your senses are stimulated beyond description as you drink in the atmosphere of the city of God.

Then you hear it—a thunderous pounding that shakes the very ground you are standing on until it feels as if you might fall. Every eye is drawn to the same opening in the vast expanse of the heavens, as through it bursts an extraordinary horse carrying the most magnificent rider you have ever seen, clothed in an almost blinding light. Stunned, you stare until every fiber of your being is drawn into a hypnotic trance at the vision before your eyes.

It is He—the One for whom you have longed, the Beloved for whom you have lived and waited. Oh, how grand He is—eyes like flaming fire, wearing a headdress adorned with shimmering jewels of every description, and a scarlet robe, the color deeper than the deepest waters you've ever known.

And then it happens—the joy for which you were created. The Bridegroom dismounts His horse and walks straight toward you, His eyes piercing your soul. You tremble as He takes your hand, and a sobering silence descends. Tenderly He places a beautiful stone in your palm. You long to look at the name you know is graven on it but you can't take your eyes away from His. Then He speaks, and it is as if you and He are utterly and astoundingly alone.

He says, "I have a name for you—it belongs to no one else, and I am the only one who knows it, for I gave it to you before the foundation of the world. You are a crown of beauty to me. You are no longer forsaken, neither is your life a desolate one, for my delight is in you and I take you now to be my own forever and ever."

Overcome by wave after wave of unfettered emotion, you can't think of a thing to say. But you don't need to, for now the heavens are swelling with song. It is the voice of the Bridegroom, and oh what a magnificent song it is! You watch in awe as He dances in sweeping, all-encompassing motion throughout the cosmos, His voice rich and full with choruses of love for you, His precious beloved. And you know that nothing else will ever move you in the same way again. Falling down, you worship the Lord, your Love, in passionate adoration.

Responding to His Call

Wait in stillness and worship before God. Spend some time offering a prayer of thanksgiving that He has made you His own. Ask Him for grace to be wholly and completely set apart, to resist anything that pulls you from His embrace.

Read Revelation 5:11–16 as a prayer of praise and worship.

Going Forward

Living in the wonder of holiness is exhilarating and humbling. To be the lover of the great I AM is mind-boggling. We will never grasp its full impact, but as God reveals His holy and passionate love for us, we can only respond with profound gratitude, falling on our face before Him. To know Him, to go hard after Him, and to live for the glory of His precious name, becomes the driving passion of our days. Let us go on to see how this simplifies every aspect of our lives.

Notes

1. Henri J. Nouwen, *Life of the Beloved* (New York: Crossroad Publishing, 1994), 106.
2. Brent Curtis and John Eldredge, *The Sacred Romance* (Nashville: Thomas Nelson Publishers, 1997), 20.
3. Alan Pronovost, from an unpublished manuscript.
4. C. S. Lewis, *Mere Christianity* (New York: MacMillan, 1952), 60.
5. Richard Foster, *Streams of Living Water* (Harper San Francisco, 1998), 83.
6. Francis Frangipane, *The Place of Immunity* (Cedar Rapids: Arrow Publications, 1994), 72.
7. A. W. Tozer, *The Knowledge of the Holy* (New York: Harper & Row, 1961), 100.
8. John Piper, *Hunger for God* (Wheaton, Ill.: Crossway Publishers, 1997), 89.
9. Edward F. Walker, *Sanctify Them* (Chicago: The Christian Witness Co., 1899), 46.
10. Gary Thomas, *Seeking the Face of God* (Nashville: Thomas Nelson Publishers, 1997), 59.
11. Phillip Yancey, *What's So Amazing About Grace?* (Grand Rapids: Zondervan, 1998), 70.

Chapter Two
SIMPLICITY

It is a Christian duty, as you know, for everyone to be
as happy as he can.[1]

C. S. Lewis

In a worn old scrapbook on a distant cousin's shelf in Denmark, I found a letter from my grandfather to his parents. Decades after having immigrated to America, he had written home, reminiscing about his childhood. The letter reflected on his Lutheran confirmation at age twelve and the three-part message given that day, which he had cherished all his life.

Through faded ink on a page yellowed with age, the words stood out like a beacon: *Never forget the brevity of life, the certainty of death, and the length of eternity.* As I read, everything suddenly seemed so simple, and I found in myself an indefinable yearning. It was the same feeling I experienced years ago when I first read the saints of old discussing detachment from this world. Their words seemed to reflect a tranquillity of soul, a kind of peacefulness that made me want to escape the chaos and complexity of my life for a simpler pilgrimage.

Simplicity is an enticing idea. It beckons us to a time when things were not so complicated, to an intangible experience we can't always find but know exists. Why? What is it we feel we've lost, and what must we relinquish in order to regain it? Does our pursuit of simplicity come primarily from a desire for balance in a world run amok with consumption? Or could it be a reflection of some deeper, hidden need? Are we, like the emperor of fairy tale lore, dressed for the parade of life in the finest money can buy but beginning to feel as if we're wearing nothing at all?

Viktor Frankl, one of this century's most brilliant and beloved psychotherapists, might suggest that the quest for simplicity is nothing more than man's search for meaning. Frankl believed that because human beings are born with a unique drive to find purpose in life, the key to our survival is the discovery of meaning in the circumstances of each day. Having survived the loss of family and the horrors of a concentration camp, Frankl concluded that man's happiness had to be found in either a cause greater than himself or a person outside himself.[2]

For most of us, simplicity means little more than a change in lifestyle that will impact the way we spend our time and use our resources. But if Frankl is right, then no amount of cutting back, scaling down, or reprioritizing schedules will ease our inner strife. A commitment to buying less will not save us from the angst of standing in front of the choices on a grocery shelf when we came for just one box of cereal. Slowing down our pace cannot keep us from being overwhelmed at the universe that invades our living room when we help our child search the Internet for some basic piece of information.

The increasing complexity of our world does not exacerbate our struggle but forces us to confront it. When we do, we soon discover that it takes more than changing our consumer ways to assuage the aspirations of our heart. A simple lifestyle does not necessarily translate into simplicity of soul.

Richard Foster tells of his own coming to terms with this reality. After doing everything in his power to compel people to simplify, he felt that in the end he was passing on one more anxiety-laden burden. He writes of his conclusion that "external acts of simplicity by themselves can be dry and artificial, producing the uneasy sense that something central is lacking."[3]

If this is so, what is it? King Solomon discovered the answer after having experienced extreme wealth, wisdom, and pleasure on this earth. He concluded that life truly is "vanity of vanities" unless men understand that God has "also set eternity in their heart" (Ecclesiastes 3:11). This desire for transcendence, or in Frankl's terms, man's search for meaning, holds the key to the "something central" lacking in most approaches to simplicity. To truly simplify, we must begin at the beginning, by asking life's deepest question: *Why am I here?*

Foundations for Simplicity

Do you ever spend time pondering the purpose of your own existence? Do you wonder why you were born to this era, into your family, with your personality and abilities? If you had asked me these questions a few years ago, in all honesty I would have had no definitive answer.

Of course, I could have (and I'm sure would have) recited an appropriate response: *I am here to serve God, to have fellowship with Him, and perhaps to prepare for eternity.* But in saying those things, I would have felt as well a weight of responsibility, the sense of destiny in my hands and fate at my fingertips. Such an approach is subtly askew for this reason: it places me at the center, an absurdity I'm only beginning to fully appreciate.

"In the beginning, God . . ." What profundity there is in this phrase, and how we miss the mark when we start from any other premise. It is only reasonable that to find the purpose for which we exist, we must begin with our source. God has always been; we are simply actors on the stage of life, created by Him, existing only because He has willed it so (Revelation 4:11). Our quest for simplicity takes form as we look within the heart of the great and mighty Maker of the universe who knows us better than we know ourselves. Thus, instead of obsessing over what might be God's will for *my life*, we must ponder a more critical question: What is *God's will*?

Jonathan Edwards, the brilliant scholar and revivalist of the eighteenth century, challenges us to begin with God, asking first why He created the world and us in it. Then we must ask how we can join Him in fulfilling *His* purposes. As we discover the answer to these two questions—*What motivates God?* and *How we can join Him in it?*—we will discover the true meaning of our lives.[4]

Why Did God Create the World and Me in It?

What motivates God? Why does He do the things He does? The first time I heard this question posed, I was struck not only with its peculiarity but also with the fact that I'd never even considered it. I had always viewed God in terms of my own sense of need—my search for significance, desire for happiness, drive for approval and acceptance, and longing for love. These were the things that motivated me. It simply had never occurred to me to ask what motivates God.

Intrigued, I began a journey that has turned my spiritual world upside down. I am eternally grateful for those who have gone before to ring the clarion call to this critical adjustment in thinking.[5] Through these and my own study of Scripture, I have come to see that since God is the origin of all things, it only follows that He must have purposes that begin not with me but with Him.

For the past several months, when teaching on prayer, I have begun by asking the participants why they think God created them. The answers usually have to do with intimacy or relationship with Him. But there is still the unasked question: *Why would He care to have intimacy or fellowship with us?* Scripture teaches that God created all things for himself: "All things have been created through Him and for Him" (Colossians 1:16). But what does this mean? Was God bored? Lonely? Did He face some inner deficiency— a longing for fellowship, as I often heard growing up?

Certainly as God He could have had no inherent need. Either He was complete in His triune nature or He wasn't God. Therefore, His incentive to create, to redeem, or to do anything must come from something that far transcends you and me. It must be something so pure, so supreme, so utterly excellent that it befits His divine nature. What could that possibly be? Only one thing—himself. God is motivated by himself—by what Scripture calls His glory. He communicates this throughout Scripture, as when He admonished the Israelites through the prophet Isaiah: "Bring My sons from afar, and My daughters from the ends of the earth, everyone who is called by My Name, and whom I have created for *My glory*, whom I have formed, even whom I have made" (Isaiah 43:6–7).

The glory of God refers to His essence, which includes His character and His ways and the manifestation of himself, and encompasses His name and reputation. God created us for His glory. Made in His image, we are to reflect His glory—the passion of our lives—back to Him and to the world around us.

Throughout Scripture we see God's glory as the motivating force behind His dealings with people. Every facet of redemption's story has the stamp of God's glory on it:

- He told the Israelites that though they had established a king against His wishes, He would not abandon them on account of His great name (1 Samuel 12:22).
- When the Israelites worshiped idols and profaned Him, God told them He would save them not for their sake but for His own, so that the nations would know He was God (Ezekiel 36:23).
- Isaiah told the Israelites that God acts for His own sake in order that His name will not be profaned and some other god receive the glory due Him (Isaiah 48:11).
- God intends to have a people whose heart's desire is His name and His memory (Isaiah 26:8).
- Although all of mankind deserved God's wrath, He patiently withheld it so that He could "make known the riches of His glory upon vessels of mercy" (Romans 9:23).
- God chose us to become His adopted children so that we would be "to the praise of the glory of His grace" (Ephesians 1:5–6).

It is a high and lofty calling to be created and chosen by the living God for His glory. Every desire we've ever known finds its fulfillment in this reality. "All our works and our words, our play and creativity, has a goal. As artists of our lives, we have a theme for our song, a motif for our painting, a point for our poem, a focus for our lives—the glory of God."[6] How we must learn to live for the day when "all the earth will be filled with the knowledge of His glory as the waters cover the sea" (Numbers 14:21; Habakkuk 2:14).

How Can I Join God in His Purposes?

After years of seeking to help others discover ways to develop intimacy with God, I have become increasingly convinced that our greatest need is not in the how-to's. I often feel frustration when trying to explain why I cannot survive for long without daily quiet times. From hard-hitting exhortation to tender pleading, I have done everything I know to do. And still people struggle, often relegating time with God to a list of spiritual requirements that they hope might become their practice at some greater level of maturity.

In a recent seminar, several had shared the usual difficulties with busyness, personal problems, and spiritual ups and downs in their attempts to be consistent in prayer. One woman spoke of emotional battles and how they kept her from coming to God. Exasperated, I tried to respond graciously: "But that's exactly why you should come. Where else can you go when you are needy?" Suddenly it was as if a light came on in my head, and I continued, "The reason we don't come to God when we're busy, or tired, or emotionally distraught is because we believe the reason we come is to give, not to get. We see a quiet time as our Christian responsibility and therefore we must 'do' it when we are strong and in good spiritual condition. But God doesn't call us to himself for what we might bring, but rather that we might know the delight of finding our deepest needs met in all that He is. What really glorifies Him are empty, needy people being filled and made whole by His goodness."

These words are a microcosm of an amazing spiritual reality. That is, that God's glory is the source of infinite gain in my life. When I come to Him in prayer, He manifests himself, commanding me to "taste and see that [He] is good" (Psalm 34:8). I meditate on His Word, crying out, "How sweet are your words to my taste! Yes, sweeter than honey to my mouth!" (Psalm 119:103). My enjoyment of Him finds even deeper fulfillment as I offer back praise and adoration—in other words, I give glory to Him. To join God in the purpose for which He created the world is to glorify Him by delighting in His wondrous character and ways.

This truth is so amazing, and yet in some ways so revolutionary, I feel inadequate to explain it. Others have said it far more eloquently. C. S. Lewis wrote, "The Scotch catechism says that man's chief end is 'to glorify God and enjoy Him forever.' But we shall then know that these are the same thing. Fully to enjoy God is to glorify Him. In commanding us to glorify Him, God is inviting us to enjoy Him."[7] Harry Kuitert wrote: "The history of Jesus makes it really clear, for the first time, that God glorifies himself not at the expense of men, but for their good. His glory means our life, our salvation, our abundance."[8]

Jonathan Edwards explained, "The happiness of the creature consists in rejoicing in God, by which also God is magnified and exalted."[9] And finally, John Piper proclaims, "The further up you go in the revealed thoughts of God, the clearer you see that God's aim in creating the world was to display the value of his own glory, and that this aim is no other than the endless, ever-increasing joy of his people in that glory."[10]

When the driving passion of our life is to find joy and delight in the pursuit of God's glory, then we have discovered our reason for being. Therefore, if the desire for simplicity reflects our very real need for meaning in life, then there is only one question to ask in all that we are, or think, or do, or feel: *How can God most be glorified?* Amazingly, in answering this, we discover how to both simplify our life and have our deepest desires fulfilled. In comparison, all other approaches seem hollow.

SIMPLICITY

A lifestyle formed by determining all things in light of the heartfelt conviction that man's chief end is to glorify God by enjoying Him forever.

Barriers to Simplicity

Years ago a Christian magazine featured an article on simplicity by a well-known Christian leader. Among other things, the author suggested that owning a Mercedes Benz could never be God's will. In a letter to the editor the following month, someone sarcastically requested that the leader provide a list of cars acceptable to God, since they weren't sure their Honda Accord made the grade.

In some ways, it would be easier if there were such a list, for then we'd "know who is in and who is out, who is faithful and who is not. Presto, a new Pharisaism."[11] But the journey with our Maker is fraught with unruly realities, one of which is that being created in His image makes us beings who must move outside the confines of regulation and rigidity to discover true joy. We are made for passion and love, emotion and experience—all things that contribute to the wonder of relationship with the living God, who displays His glory in and around us.

Perhaps the greatest barrier to simplicity is that we just keep asking the wrong questions. Simplicity is not found in determining what we can or can't do, or should or should not have, but in discovering how to make God's glory preeminent in the little things as well as the large. Then our joy will expand, opening wide the horizons His glory demands. We are hindered in this quest when we settle for lesser goals than God's glory, underestimate the worth of His glory, or fail to make it central in our lives.

We Settle for Lesser Goals Than God's Glory

Recently our family took a road trip from our home in San Diego to central Colorado. As we crossed the California desert into the wide-open spaces of Nevada, there was little to see. Several miles outside of Las Vegas, we were inundated with bright flashing billboards advertising the glories of that gambling Mecca. Promises of fun, fortune, and fulfillment, from sign after sign, provided a powerful allure.

Clever architecture and grandiose edifices beckoned us to come in as the freeway took us through the heart of the city. From replicas of the Statue of Liberty and the Leaning Tower of Pisa to a roller coaster spinning atop the tallest building, our senses were assaulted with an appeal to pleasure. We were dumbfounded as hotels competed for our attention by flaunting multicolored facades and dazzling light shows.

A few hours later we reached Zion National Park, our destination for that day. Here too we were taken aback at what we saw, but this time it was the grandeur of God's creation that astounded us. Nothing in my life's experiences could have prepared me for being surrounded by the stark beauty of those two-to-three-thousand-foot cliffs. Words simply cannot describe the vast and varied expressions of God's handiwork in that place. From towering rock formations that loomed like decorated soldiers at attention to sandy plateaus etched with line upon variegated line of every imaginable hue, we were stunned into silence.

That evening the day appeared to me a study in contrasts. Contemplating the beauty that now filled my view, Las Vegas with all its pretentious finery seemed tawdry and tainted. I was struck with sadness at the reality that every year thousands upon thousands of people stop just a few hours short of Zion—an experience infinitely more glorious than the passing pleasures Las Vegas could ever bring.

This illustrates in a powerful way what Scripture calls sin. "For all have sinned and fall short of the glory of God" (Romans 3:23). The word for "fall short" in Greek means "to be inferior" or "to lack."[12] Thus the greatest tragedy of life is settling for an inferior purpose and lesser call than the glory of God, or, in other words, stopping in Las Vegas when we could go on to Zion National Park.

All sin can be seen as the "suicidal exchange of infinite value and beauty for some fleeting inferior substitute."[13] If we truly desire simplicity, we must look at things like the house we want or the way we spend our free time, by asking, *Am I settling for a temporal pleasure here when my longings reflect a need for something far greater?* Consider the following scenarios:

- A man buys a motorcycle and ends up spending weekend after weekend on the road, away from the fellowship of believers. The question isn't whether it is right or wrong, or even a bad expenditure, but whether he is settling for the thrill of the ride when he could be experiencing the glory God pours out upon His people in worship.
- A teenage girl falls in love, becoming sexually active. Is she settling for physical affection or the security of belonging to someone when she could be experiencing the love of God, who manifests His glory in deep and satisfying spiritual intimacy with His beloved followers?
- A businessman climbs the corporate ladder, working seventy-hour weeks year after year. Is he settling for the applause of this world when He could be experiencing the glory of God through the beauty of marital bliss and the wonder of his children's growth and development?

Often we feel guilty at the ways we amass material possessions, or we are weary with the insane busyness of life, but we can't find a way out. The idea of a simpler lifestyle appeals to us, but our efforts don't seem to make much difference. The problem is that we are not really living for God's glory.

We are in sin, "falling short" of the only thing that can fill us with joy and bring meaningful balance to the issues of life. Our only solution is to go hard after God, settling for nothing but the experience of all that He is in everything that touches us.

When we do, our lifestyle will inevitably change. We will no longer be compelled to pursue possessions and experiences, because the void we have sought to fill will have been met in a far greater way. Having and doing less is the result of true simplicity, not the means of gaining it as we may have once thought.

We Underestimate the Worth of God's Glory

The completely fulfilling manifestation of God's glory is revealed in His Son, Jesus Christ: "And the Word became flesh, and dwelt among us, and we saw His glory, glory as of the only begotten from the Father, full of grace and truth" (John 1:14). The author of Hebrews tells us that Jesus is the radiance of the Father's glory and upholds all things by the word of His power. Because of this, "when He had made purification of sins, He sat down at the right hand of the Majesty on high" (Hebrews 1:3). The reign of Jesus Christ was made possible in the hearts of men through His death on the cross. Anyone born of the Spirit, therefore, enters a spiritual reality called the kingdom of God (John 3:5).

Jesus likened the discovery of His kingdom to someone tripping over an unknown gold mine in an empty field. Leaping for joy, he rushes off to sell everything in order to buy it. What has he really discovered? What has so filled him with joy that the treasures of this world suddenly taste like sawdust in his mouth? The answer is a profound mystery. The kingdom of God is the rule of the King of Kings and the Lord of Lords. It is the realm in which the eternal Jehovah reigns in all His glory. Simply put, when we enter the kingdom of God, we enter a domain in which God's character and ways are supreme. Because He is infinitely perfect, it is a perfect kingdom.

This is what we were created for and what we lost through sin. It is that which our souls crave most desperately and the answer to every desire for happiness we could ever have. When Christ takes His rightful place on the throne of our hearts, we are granted every privilege of kingdom status. We inherit the glories of a King who does all things well and will not deny us the joy of His presence. His kingdom is an everlasting kingdom and we will live in the wonder of His flawless rule for eternity.

Our failure to live for the glory of God, to pursue Christ's reign over every part of our life, is an indication that we do not realize what He offers us. The things of this world are cheap imitations that lose their luster in the light of God's kingdom. When we know this—truly know it—like Paul we will count everything in this world as loss and rubbish (Philippians 3:10).

If we find ourselves unwilling to suffer to gain Christ, or if our plans, our pleasures, and our investments in the things of this world have an irresistible appeal to our hearts, then we simply have not experienced the glory of Christ's reign. His rule so far surpasses those things that there is really no basis for comparison. When we know the joy of obedience to our glorious King, we will cry out that to live is Christ and to die is to gain greater depths of this eternal treasure (Philippians 1:21).

We Don't Make God's Glory Central

Recently a neighbor for whom I have prayed for several months was watering her lawn as I went to my mailbox. Though I had asked God often to provide opportunities to connect with her, that day I stood at my curb debating whether or not I had time to walk over. As I thought about it later, I wondered why I resisted. I think it has something to do with how I live out God's call on my life. Though I say I want God to be glorified, times like these remind me I am not living for the glory of God, it is not the central factor of my life at the moment.

Jesus told us to seek *first* the kingdom of God (Matthew 6:33). We tend to think this means to put God at the top of the list, saying things like *God first, family second, work or ministry third,* and on down. But this approach compartmentalizes our lives and puts us in danger of leaving God out of major sections simply by default. Like my dilemma at my mailbox, we live for all practical purposes as if God has little place outside of the "God category."

When Jesus said "first," He used the word *protos*, meaning "supreme" or "first in time, place, order, and importance."[14] In other words, the reign of our glorious God is not only at the top of the list but it is also the central factor in everything on our list—it is the hub around which all else must revolve. We cannot set aside or categorize God's reign, for it is ever in effect, always accomplishing His eternal purpose to glorify himself.

When we understand this, everything that happens—whether an hour in prayer, a softball game with our kid's Little League, a job in a new town, or a neighbor at the mailbox—has significance. We do not simply "pass rudderless from one episode to another, idly seeking some distraction to pass the time."[15] Living in awareness and wonder of this reality is critical to enjoying the simplicity God wills for our lives.

What We Must Do

The difficulty with having such a lofty basis as the glory of God to define the living of life is in finding a practical way of working it out—like the old adage "We can be so heavenly minded we're no earthly good." But the glory of God is immensely practical, a fact evidenced by the abundance of Christ's teaching on money and possessions. Once we've done away with the rigidity of rules for simplifying our life, then we can purposefully consider the question *How then shall we live?*

God's Glory for Today: The Gain of Intimate Relationship

To make practical decisions about simplifying, we must be compelled by motivation that goes beyond shoulds and should-nots. We need to see as God sees, think as He thinks, and make decisions from His perspective, His glory radiating into all we do. God gave us a wonderful plan to make this happen—a plan called *relationship*. Eternal life is in essence *knowing Him* intimately (John 17:3).

Moses walked with God as a friend, and when He showed him His glory, Moses cried out that He was a God who was "compassionate and gracious, slow to anger, and abounding in lovingkindness and truth; who keeps lovingkindness for thousands, who forgives iniquity, transgression and sin; yet He will by no means leave the guilty unpunished" (Exodus 34:6–7). When the glory of God fell upon the Israelites at the dedication of Solomon's temple, they fell to the ground in worship for they saw that God is "good, truly His lovingkindness is everlasting" (2 Chronicles 7:3). David spent hours with His Lord in the temple, calling it the place where God's glory dwelt. He cried out in awe, "I have seen you in the sanctuary, to see your power and your glory" (Psalm 26:8; 63:2).

Over and over in Scripture when God's glory is mentioned, we learn something about Him. Thus to discover God's glory is really to know and commune with Him in ever-increasing intimacy. This does not happen automatically, but without it our lives cannot ascend to the level He desires for us. If we do not meet with God in the depths of our soul, it is unlikely we will experience and live for His glory in the expanse of the universe or the humdrum of daily existence.

This is the profound motivation for contemplative or quiet prayer. In stillness we learn to wait on the living God, who is ever committed to reveal His glory to us. Because He is infinite and dwells in unapproachable light, our relationship with Him can never be confined to quiet-time formulas and practical prayer pointers.

God condescends to unveil himself to man. Can you feel the weight of such a thing? He has "shown in our hearts to give the light of the knowledge of the glory of God in the face of Christ" (2 Corinthians 4:6). This is truly unfathomable, and we can only respond by devoting our life on this earth and into eternity to exploring the wonder of His Being.[16] From the marvel of intimacy in God's presence to the mundane details of life, our eyes can be opened to His glory.

What does this have to do with the issues we normally associate with a simpler lifestyle? How does intimacy with God impact the clothes I buy or the house I live in? This has become a driving question for me. Having spent some time in developing countries, I am continually concerned that my way of life is formed more by my culture than the will of God. This dilemma has forced me to spend much time in prayer over these things.

In the end, intimacy with my Lord means that I can no longer just go along with what the world says is the way to live. I must continually ask the hard questions. The answers may differ for you and for me with regard to material possessions, but God wants to walk with us: guiding, rebuking, and changing our hearts. I feel great hope when I see that He has taken away my love for things I once thought indispensable and opened my eyes to the emptiness of this world's values concerning affluence and success. He will show each of us how He wants us to live, and intimacy with Him means we are always turning to Him, seeking His counsel, loving the journey He is taking us on.

When we live with the longing to discover God's glory, every day becomes an incredible adventure, for we never know when He will break into the ordinary to do some extraordinary thing. This is the joy of continual communion with Him—who would want to miss any part of it? We can settle for nothing less once we've tasted such a life, crying out as David did, "My mouth is filled with your praise and with your glory all day long" (Psalm 71:8).

God's Glory for Tomorrow: The Gain of Eternal Investments

That God grants us the privilege of relationship on this earth is an amazing thing—a gain grand enough to change our entire way of living. But Paul says that if we have hoped in Christ in this life only, we of all people are most to be pitied (1 Corinthians 15:19). Incredibly, there is more. This incomprehensible God we serve actually desires and enables us to live on this earth in such a way that will bring us even greater gain in eternity. This motivation can transcend all others, for our life here is but a breath, while eternity is . . . forever!

Like most people, simplicity has often been for me a mandate to cut back, let go of material things, and slow down. When God first began speaking to my heart about worldly values, these were the kinds of changes I made. I bought used clothes, kept things until they wore out, eliminated unnecessary busyness, learned to say no, bought with cash instead of credit, and many other things. I believe these were all good, but they did not reflect God's profound will for my eternal future.

Simplicity is not about *divesting* but about *investing*. Every time Jesus warns us about the treasures of this world, it is in the context of what we have to gain in the world to come. This means it is ludicrous to admire missionaries for their sacrifice when instead we should envy the great inheritance they are storing up for themselves. Why would we feel badly for the rich young ruler who is told to sell all, when we know that Jesus promised in return, "You will have treasure in heaven" (Matthew 19:21)?

We are created to want more, to desire something glorious and grand, and no amount of denying this will change it. The problem is we settle for the limited pleasures of this world, demonstrating that our desires are as C. S. Lewis wrote, "not too strong but too weak."[17] Jesus continually calls us to pursue the gain of eternal investments so that we won't be trapped by the futility of a world that is passing away. Randy Alcorn, in his book *Money, Eternity, and Possessions*, clarifies this:

> We must realize Jesus didn't tell us we are wrong in wanting to lay up treasures. On the contrary, he commanded us to lay up treasures. He was simply saying, "Stop laying them up in the wrong place, and start laying them up in the right place." Christ's primary argument against amassing material wealth was not that it was bad,

but simply that it was a poor investment.[18]

Whatever this world might give: status, success, glamour, wealth, or pleasure, God offers something far greater—an inheritance that is imperishable and undefiled and will not fade away (1 Peter 1:4). Moses gave up his lofty role as Pharaoh's son because he was looking to his reward (Hebrews 11:26). The early Christians joyfully relinquished their homes and all that they owned, for they knew they had a better and lasting possession awaiting them (Hebrews 10:34). God has blessed us with an incredible life on this earth, but He did not intend that it should capture our affections.

This, of course, is easier said than done. How do we live day after day in this world and not become ensnared by it, being *in* but not *of* it? How can we maintain balance when the car breaks down, or our family gets too big for the house we live in? Jesus understood these difficulties. After admonishing the crowd in the Sermon on the Mount about the futility of trying to serve both God and wealth, He adds, "For this reason I say to you, do not be worried about your life" (Matthew 6:25). The word "worried" can be translated "distracted."[19] He counsels us not to be distracted about food or clothing—the basics of life.

Often we quote this passage for its beautiful promise that God will meet our physical needs as surely as He feeds the sparrow and clothes the lily. But I believe Jesus had a broader purpose in His words. Three times He refers to the brevity of life on this earth:

1. "Is not life more than food and the body more than clothing?"

2. "And who of you by being worried can add a single hour to his life?"

3. "But if God so clothes the grass of the field, which is alive today and tomorrow is thrown into the furnace, will He not much more do so for you?"

It seems Jesus is saying that as long as we live on this earth, He will provide what we need. Therefore, we are not to be so distracted by those things that we forget our real destiny.

Floyd McClung, veteran YWAM missionary, tells that when God called him back to the United States to begin a mission training school, he found himself following the advice of others to plan for his retirement. He studied, worked on a portfolio, and sought to prepare for the future, but one day God revealed that the whole thing was distracting him from his real purpose. He related in a message to our church:

> As I thought about it, it just didn't make sense to spend so much time and energy on this. My wife and I talked for a while and concluded that the worst thing that could happen is we would starve to death. They say it only takes thirty-some days to die of starvation and I'd rather leave this world that way than waste my hours trying to cover bases I may never get to.

Isn't it amazing that we find his decision so radical in light of Jesus' admonitions to store up treasure in heaven and Paul's words to be content with food and covering (Matthew 6:19–20; 1 Timothy 6:8)? We say we're a people of the Word, but do we really believe its outrageous claims and commands? Sadly, we ignore these passages and dozens of others and, in fact, live in direct opposition to them. By our lives, it appears we think it is our destiny to accumulate here, to find comfort in this world. We expend countless hours and huge amounts of money to guarantee this.

This is one reason simplicity sounds so appealing. We've been endlessly enticed into owning more and more in order to make our lives more comfortable. But the more we own, the more time we must spend maintaining it, and in the end every day becomes increasingly complex—all because we believe it incumbent upon ourselves to make life easier and avoid suffering of any kind.

Such an approach flies in the face of the thousands in the persecuted church who are tortured and killed every day for their faith in Christ. What in the world compels them to tolerate such treacherous conditions, while we deplore the irritation of a house without air conditioning or disdain a suit that is no longer in style?

Paul, a veteran of affliction, dismisses the question out of hand, saying, "I consider that the sufferings of this present time are not worthy to be compared with the glory that is to be revealed to us" (Romans 8:18). In fact, he saw his trials as a blessing, only increasing his investment in eternity. He wrote to the Corinthian church, "For momentary, light affliction is producing for us an eternal weight of glory far beyond all comparison, while we look not at the things which are seen, but at the things which are not seen; for the things which are seen are temporal, but the things which are not seen are eternal" (2 Corinthians 4:17–18).

Oh, that we might comprehend what awaits us beyond the pale of this world. How we need to pray with fervency that the eyes of our heart might be enlightened to know what is the hope of His calling and the riches of the glory of His inheritance (Ephesians 1:18). If we grasped even a glimpse of what this means, we would be always rejoicing at the revelation of His glory, celebrating the day we will stand in the "presence of His glory blameless, with great joy" (Jude 1:24).

In Quest of Simplicity

In his early years, before God changed his heart and sent him to spread the gospel in Burma, Adoniram Judson envisioned himself pastoring a large, prestigious church. But one night he had a dream in which he saw his father, an obscure country pastor, in heaven. Suddenly he knew how deceived he'd been. He wrote of what he saw: "The world was wrong about its heroes. The world was wrong in its judgments. The fame of the unknown country pastor was really the greater—so much greater that any worldly accomplishment shrank into insignificance. This was the only fame that triumphed over the grave."[20]

Decades later on his deathbed, after having sacrificed everything this world might hold dear, Judson said he felt like a young bride who contemplates leaving the pleasant memories of her childhood for yet a dearer home.

He could not wait to experience the reward he'd spent a lifetime preparing for.

What a wondrous thought—not only do we walk in intimacy with the God of glory but we will also one day stand before Him to receive the reward He has promised. Listen to His voice: "Behold, I am coming quickly, and My reward is with Me, to render to every man according to what he has done. I am the Alpha and the Omega, the first and the last, the beginning and the end" (Revelation 22:12–13).

With this reality we have come full circle. *In the beginning . . . God.* He is the first and last—His glory supreme above all other glories. All that we do must be evaluated in light of the reality that one day we will stand before this King of Kings whose glory we will then fully see. C. S. Lewis wrote of the wonder of such a thing:

> It is written that we shall "stand before" Him, shall appear, shall be inspected. The promise of glory is the promise, almost incredible and only possible by the work of Christ, that some of us, that any of us who really chooses, shall actually survive that examination, shall find approval, shall please God. To please God . . . to be a real ingredient in the divine happiness . . . to be loved by God, not merely pitied, but delighted in as an artist delights in his work or a father in a son—it seems impossible, a weight or burden of glory which our thoughts can hardly sustain. But so it is.[21]

How I long to live for God's voice saying, "Well done, good and faithful servant." Could anything be more glorious? This is the heart of simplicity. Anything else is a shortsighted substitute.

TAKING UP OUR CROSS—
What We Gain and What We Lose

When the glory of God is the central pursuit of our lives, we welcome each day as another step in the journey. Regardless of our circumstances, we know that our almighty God is at work, for we are looking to the heavenly realm where all things are in subjection to Christ. But when our focus is this world, we are bothered by change and thrown by difficult situations. Always fearful and uncertain of what might happen next, we can never really rest.

Gain Confident Assurance

"For this reason I also suffer these things, but I am not ashamed; for I know whom I have believed and I am convinced that He is able to guard what I have entrusted to Him until that day" (2 Timothy 1:12).

Lose Uncertainty

"Instruct those who are rich in this present world not to be conceited or to fix their hope on the uncertainty of riches, but on God, who richly supplies us with all things to enjoy" (1 Timothy 6:17).

People spend scores of hours and a tremendous amount of emotional energy for a future that depends entirely on the often-capricious nature of the stock market or the investment skills of some willing counselor. But there are no guarantees, and even when success comes, the rewards are transient and unfulfilling. How wonderful instead, to know that our investments in the kingdom of God are sure, our rewards guaranteed by His righteous Word.

Gain Eternal Rewards

"But store up for yourselves treasures in heaven, where neither moth nor rust destroys, and where thieves do not break in or steal; for where your treasure is, there your heart will be also" (Matthew 6:20–21).

Lose Unprofitable Investments

"Every goldsmith is put to shame by his idols; for his molten images are deceitful, and there is no breath in them. They are worthless, a work of mockery" (Jeremiah 10:14–15).

Following Christ feels like one more life duty when we try to add it to the fast-paced agenda most of us have. We labor to do the right things but miss the peace of His presence. We are at the mercy of everyone else's opinion about how to follow Jesus, for we haven't learned the joy of walking with Him in single-minded devotion. When we do, we know His voice and give Him alone the right to rule in our hearts. Daily His Spirit infuses us with supernatural strength and fervent inner determination.

Gain Stamina

"Brethren, I do not regard myself as having laid hold of it yet; but one thing I do: forgetting what lies behind and reaching forward to what lies ahead, I press on toward the goal for the prize of the upward call of God in Christ Jesus" (Philippians 3:13–14).

Lose Weariness/Burnout

"For what does a man get in all his labor and in his striving with which he labors under the sun? Because all his days his task is painful and grievous; even at night his mind does not rest. This too is vanity" (Ecclesiastes 2:22–23).

Often we feel torn in a hundred directions. Every decision is a tyrant at our door, and we have no sense of clarity. Outwardly we keep our lives intact, but inside we are fragmented and ill equipped to plan even one day in advance. Simplicity of soul solves this by narrowing every decision down to one question: *How is God most glorified?* When we operate under this framework, we find a depth of purpose in all we do.

Gain Focus

"Everyone who competes in the games exercises self-control in all things. They then do it to receive a perishable wreath, but we an imperishable. Therefore, I run in such a way, as not without aim; I box in such a way, as not beating the air" (1 Corinthians 9:25–26).

Lose Fragmentation

"If a kingdom is divided against itself, that kingdom cannot stand. If a house is divided against itself, that house will not be able to stand" (Mark 3:24–25).

To pursue God's glory is to pursue intimacy with Him, for this is His desire. When we know Him as Father and Lover, it is easy to give Him His rightful place of Lord in the habitation of our heart. As we do, we experience a blessed serenity deep within. But when we make serving rather than seeking our primary goal, instead of spiritual reward we experience stress-filled lives.

Gain Serenity

"For the kingdom of God is not eating and drinking, but righteousness and peace and joy in the Holy Spirit" (Romans 14:17).

"For the mind set on the flesh is death, but the mind set on the Spirit is life and peace" (Romans 8:6).

Lose Stress

"But Martha was distracted with all her preparations; and she came up to Him, and said, 'Lord, do You not care that my sister has left me to do all the serving alone? Then tell her to help me.' But the Lord answered and said to her, 'Martha, Martha, you are worried and bothered about so many things; but only one thing is necessary, for Mary has chosen the good part, which shall not be taken away from her'" (Luke 10:40–42).

Oh, how glorious the gain when we determine to die to the desires of this world and live for God's glory. To be *of* the world can only result in a life of uncertainty, unprofitable investments, burnout, fragmentation, and stress—why would we ever cling to such things? Let us take up our cross against them as God infuses our soul with confidence, stamina, purpose, serenity, and the expectation of great reward that comes from enjoying God, whose glory has become our driving passion.

PRACTICING SIMPLICITY—
A Mini-Retreat

In the midst of a very busy world and after a season of intense ministry, Jesus called for His disciples to withdraw with Him to a secluded place so they could rest awhile (Mark 6:31). How we need to make this the practice of our lives as well. The pace of our lives today makes it almost impossible for us to really evaluate things if we don't stop now and then to shut everything down to listen to God's voice. This is the purpose of this time in His presence.

Preparing Your Heart

As you quiet your own soul, hear the voice of Jesus speaking to you directly:

"Come away by yourself to a secluded place and rest awhile." The disciples had just returned from their first evangelistic outreach where they went from city to city preaching, casting out demons, and anointing people with oil for healing. Jesus knew their need to pull away. As you wait before Him, release all the things that you have been busy with in the past days—let it all go. Hear Him say once again, "Come away by yourself to a secluded place and rest awhile."

Read Revelation 21:10–11 and 21–27 quietly and reflectively. Consider the wonder of the time when God's glory will illumine all things. Take some time to thank Him for having written your name in His Book of Life. Worship Him as King of Kings and Lord of Lords. Write a prayer of praise in your journal.

Contemplating His Presence

Read Luke 9:57–62 and 18:20–22 as you open your heart to allow God to reveal His glory to you in a new way.

When we read of Jesus' offering common men the simple invitation to "follow Me," we see some who held too tightly to what they had, and could not respond. Others, though, recklessly abandoned everything to go with Him. Nets full of fish drifting out to sea and empty tax collectors' booths gave radiant testimony to the reality that for some, Christ held out something worth leaving everything for.

Efforts to simplify our life based on giving something up will never provide enduring spiritual change. Our only hope is an overwhelming experience of discovery—to see something we've never seen before and be so taken with it that everything else fades in significance. Ask God to show you these things with spiritual eyes as you experience the following contemplation. Read it through once or twice, then prayerfully place yourself in it.

> *Time for bed again. As you hit the pillow, you long for sleep to come quickly. Instead, your head begins to pound and your mind races mercilessly with endless unrelated details.*
>
> *Things should not be as they are—of this you are sure. You feel a bit guilty, knowing that others would say you have it made, but they are more impressed than you are with the life you live. Though there is little you need, day after day you work longer and longer hours. For what?* you say. *Who knows why? What else can I do?*
>
> *Lately you just can't get away from a gnawing restlessness deep inside that tells you something is wrong. But you don't really have time to find*

out what it is. All you can do is keep going; continue doing what you've always done. You should be happy—a maxim you repeat to yourself every night as you drift off to a fitful sleep.

And so ends another day. But this time a dream fills your subconscious mind almost instantly. It is a vivid one, full of color and feeling and life. You see yourself walking down the middle of a long road toward what looks like a gate in the distance. It's hard to know what lies beyond, but something oddly delightful seems to be pulling you toward it.

Puzzled, you turn to look around. The road behind you is lined with things that compete for your attention. On your left, you see your house, and you feel a sense of pride welling up at its beauty. Then, feeling the familiar stress about its cracked foundation and leaky faucets, you look away. You are relieved when you see your car—at least there's nothing wrong with that. It's a little extravagant, but you've dreamed of owning one like it since college. As you stare at it, though, the thought of monthly payments and upkeep settles over you like a dark cloud, increasing your anxiety.

You catch a slight movement on the road beside you. How strange that your boss is here! He laughs as he throws an arm around your shoulder, patting you on the back. But something doesn't feel right—his hand is like a crushing weight. Compelled to look forward again, you remember the gate. What is there about it that makes you want to break loose and run toward it with all your might?

With a little trepidation, you glance back again, this time to your right. It looks like some kind of party is going on—you see your college roommate, your trainer from the gym, and the teller from your bank. They call out for you to join them. They look like they're having a lot of fun, but for some reason your heart begins to pound in your chest.

Everything in you wants to go forward, but your feet seem to be glued to the road and you can't move. As you look again to the gate in the distance, a light emanates from it with a brilliance and warmth that stirs you deeply. A passion to be caught up in its glow swells within you. You can't remember ever wanting anything as much as you want this now.

Trying to drag one leg in front of the other, you glance back and are horrified to see that all the things on the road behind you have become traps of one type or another. They are snapping at you like hungry jaws.

With all the strength you can muster, you propel yourself forward toward the light; a primal cry escapes your innermost being. Your feet begin to move—slowly at first, then a little faster. Then a strange thing happens. You find yourself leaping, your feet barely touching the ground. You are buoyant, almost airborne.

The light and warmth is within reach now . . . drawing you forward— closer . . . closer. . . . Just as you get to the gate, it flings wide open and you are drawn into the most glorious experience you have ever known. It is magnificent here. Sinking to your knees, you worship the living God, whose glory fills everything for as far as you can see with a brilliance and beauty beyond anything words can describe.

Peace enfolds you as you finally understand that this is all that life is worth living for, giving your all for. The road behind you, cluttered now with the debris of empty lives, seems fruitless when compared to the wonder of what you have found. You are aware of only one thought: You must do whatever it takes to stay in this place, for nothing you've ever known can compare to it.

Responding to His Call

Spend some time contemplating the things that might be on the road if you were to have this dream. In prayer, offer each one up to God, asking Him to show you the incredible gain of living for His glory instead of for those things. Rest quietly once again in His presence.

Read Psalm 24:7–10 aloud in praise to God. See the gates as the entrance into your heart of hearts and the doors as the way into all the parts of your life. Rejoice that He enters as King, that the kingdom of God has come in all its glory to fill your life.

Going Forward

God is motivated by His own glory and will accomplish His purposes concerning it whether we give ourselves to Him or not. But we have the incredible privilege of joining Him and enjoying the privileges His glory bestows. As we come to know the character and ways of this consummate King, we will experience a deep sense of well-being concerning every part of our life. Contentment will radiate from our heart to the world around us. Let us seek to gain this most blessed state of being.

Notes

1. Sheldon Vanauken, *A Severe Mercy* (New York: Harper & Row, 1977), 189. (From a personal letter from Lewis to Vanauken.)
2. See Viktor Frankl, *Man's Search for Meaning* (New York: Pocket Books, Washington Square Press, 1998).
3. Richard J. Foster, *Simplicity* (New York: Harper & Row, 1981), 46.
4. See John Piper, *God's Passion for His Glory*, an exposition on Jonathan Edwards' book *The End for Which God Created the World* (Wheaton, Ill.: Crossway Books, 1998).
5. Jonathan Edwards, C. S. Lewis, and today John Piper, have written extensively on this subject. If these thoughts are fresh to you, you may want to begin with Piper's classic, *Desiring God*.
6. Don Postema, *Space for God* (Grand Rapids: CRC Publications, 1997), 185.
7. C. S. Lewis, *Reflections on the Psalms* (New York: Harcourt Brace, Inc., 1964), 94.
8. Harry M. Kuitert; Lewis B. Smedes, trans., *Signals From the Bible* (Grand Rapids: William B. Eerdmans Publishing Co., 1972), 94.
9. As quoted in John Piper, *God's Passion for His Glory* (Wheaton, Ill.: Crossway Books, 1998), 47.
10. Piper, 32.
11. Foster, 8.
12. *Strong's Concordance* definition, electronic database, 1996 Biblesoft.
13. Piper, 43.
14. *Strong's Concordance*.

15. Brennan Manning, *Abba's Child* (Colorado Springs: NavPress, 1994), 110.
16. For help in the journey of contemplative prayer, see my books *The Soul at Rest: A Journey Into Contemplative Prayer* (1996) and *Contemplating the Cross: A Pilgrimage of Prayer* (1998), both by Bethany House Publishers.
17. C. S. Lewis, *The Weight of Glory and Other Addresses* (New York: Simon & Schuster, 1965), 26.
18. Randy Alcorn, *Money, Eternity, and Possessions* (Wheaton, Ill.: Tyndale House Publishers, 1989), 125.
19. *Strong's Concordance*.
20. Courtney Anderson, *To the Golden Shore: The Life of Adoniram Judson* (Boston: Little, Brown, and Company, 1956), 29.
21. Lewis, 34.

CHAPTER THREE

CONTENTMENT

*There is a spot deep within our souls that is hungry and not being fed.
There is a place in our hearts that is thirsty, and no one gives us to
drink. There is a naked corner of our spirits
that no one offers to clothe.*[1]

R. C. Sproul

We, the church of Jesus Christ in America, are a people of paradox. Perhaps never in history has Christianity known such free reign, nor its adherents so little oppression. In the land of plenty, there is a church for every personality, and if our needs or desires change, we can always try another. Our Christian bookstores stock materials for our most obscure wants and music for every mood we face. Bible studies and workshops abound—we can dine at a smorgasbord of truth on any given evening without leaving home, thanks to TV, radio, and the Internet.

Yet in the angst-filled stillness of a sleepless night, many who claim faith in Christ are aware of a "roving and indestructible discontent—a feeling that life is not what it ought to be."[2] Fearful of exposing our raw and perhaps painful condition, we've learned well how to busy ourselves until the malaise lies safely dormant at the back of our minds.

Sometimes, though, when we fail to contain it, our discontent erupts, manifesting itself in a multitude of "if onlys." If only I had a different job. If only my parents had loved me more. If only my church had more life. If only I were healthy. If only my wife understood me. If only my pastor were more caring. If only our house were a little bigger or our car a little nicer or our computer a little faster . . . on and on the list goes and grows.

Why, in the midst of unprecedented abundance, would some feel such great lack? Why do many swim in a sea of discontent when the Good News we proclaim teaches that believers should be the most satisfied people in the world? Why this disconnect between what *ought to be* and what really *is* in the depths of our souls?

The author of Hebrews gives perhaps the most definitive word on contentment in Scripture. In a letter of encouragement to young believers who had sold all they had to support their imprisoned loved ones, he wrote, "Let your way of life be free from the love of money, being content with what you have, for He Himself has said, 'I will never leave you nor forsake you' " (Hebrews 13:5).

The Greek root word for "content" (*arkeo*) means "sufficient" or "enough." Thus, according to God's Word, contentment comes from knowing that God is enough, from experiencing His sufficiency, resting in the reality that He will never leave us. If we are not content, if He isn't enough for us, then what conclusion can we draw? Where is our hope? Is the problem with God or with us?

A. W. Tozer, one of the most compelling prophets of the twentieth century, would say the problem certainly is not with God but instead is rooted in our distorted view of Him. In his final years Tozer wrote a profound treatise addressing the state of the church—a sickly condition that he says formed slowly and without her knowledge:

> The Church has surrendered her once lofty concept of God and has substituted it for one so low, so ignoble, as to be utterly unworthy of thinking, worshiping men. . . . This God we have made, and because we have made him we can understand him; because we have created him he can never surprise us, never overwhelm us, nor astonish us, nor transcend us.[3]

If our God is not sufficient to meet our deepest yearnings, then it is not the God of the Scriptures but a god we have created according to our own wants and experiences—in essence, an idol of the heart. What might this god of our own making look like? If we were to form an opinion based on the sermons preached across the land or the books bought by believers over the past twenty years, it might bear some resemblance to the following:

- A god more consumed with our personal problems than with his own glory.
- A god who does not break into our lives in astonishing power and thus does not elicit fearful awe.
- A god who sits in heaven stressed over lost souls, begging us to reach them.
- An inept god who must leave us to human wisdom to solve the problems of our life.
- A god at our beck and call, giving us health, wealth, and prosperity to prove he loves us.
- A god who keeps score of religious works, rewarding us when we do well and punishing us when we fail.
- A god whose love for us is based on our worth—who can't help but love us because we are so special.
- A god who doesn't mind if we get a little of his glory as long as we're acting in his name.
- A god who blinks at sin or will change his nature to ensure our happiness.
- A god for whom we are the center of his universe.

The list could go on, and you might add a few or take some away. The writer of Psalm 115 paints a graphic picture of the inevitable result of making a god in our own image. He says it will have a mouth that can't speak, eyes that can't see, ears that can't hear, a nose that can't smell, hands that can't feel, and feet that can't walk. Then he offers the stunning conclusion: "Those who make them will become like them" (Psalm 115:8). Herein lies perhaps the impotence in our souls. We have unwittingly become like the gods we've created, gods that bear little resemblance to the character and ways of the living God.

The infinite Alpha and Omega, King of Kings, Lord of Lords, eternal Father, and Creator of all things condescends to reveal himself to man. It is this God who pledges that He will never—He will *never* leave. How could knowing El Shaddai (God almighty) not cause our hearts to pulse with profound hope? Could He ever be less than enough? Shouldn't intimacy with Adonai (my Lord) produce a sense of well-being so deep that nothing would shake the satisfaction that fills our souls?

The lives of those who have gone before us affirm without question that God is more than adequate for every need we could ever face. We see a grief-ridden prophet named Jeremiah, who in the face of national and personal destruction, concluded: "The Lord is my portion. . . . Therefore I have hope in Him" (Lamentations 3:24). We hear David's song reverberating from the walls of a cave where he hid in fear for his life: "Delight yourself in the Lord and He will give you the desires of your heart" (Psalm 37:4). We wonder at a watchman named Habakkuk, who with trembling stomach at the distress to come vowed:

> Though the fig tree should not blossom and there be no fruit on the vines, though the yield of the olive should fail and the fields produce no food, though the flock should be cut off from the fold and there be no cattle in the stalls, yet I will exult in the Lord, I will rejoice in the God of my salvation. (Habakkuk 3:17–18)

From the beginning of time, those who walked with God have affirmed His ultimate and absolute sufficiency.

☙ ☙

CONTENTMENT

A deep sense of well-being that comes from experiencing God as the all-satisfying One.

Foundations for Contentment

The infinite God of the universe pursues us, draws our hearts to His, and takes us into the secret places of His own heart that we might know Him. If this truth ever takes hold of us, we'll never recover from an acute sense of awe. How we need to lay aside faulty and worthless conceptions of a vapid god who cannot meet our deepest needs, and to cry out for a vision of the living God's glory. When He gives us even a taste of who He is, the reality that He made us for himself and ever lives to satisfy our souls will rock our hearts and revolutionize our lives.

Crying Out for a Vision of God's Glory

At the dawn of a new millennium a call is growing throughout our land for a reformation—not on the scale of Luther's, but perhaps as desperately needed. It is a call to recapture the grandeur of the God who has redeemed us for His glory. Multitudes in the church today are bound by a man-centered infatuation with a god formed from their personal experience instead of the truth of His Word.

The God of Scripture cannot be contained, explained, managed, or negotiated with. He is the Most High God, worthy of worship and honor at all times from the lips of fallen man. He is inscrutable, inexplicable, unspeakable, unutterable, and ineffable. He transcends us at every point.

Often God's Word seeks to define Him in terms we can relate to, but even then our minds fail to grasp the magnitude of His greatness. Isaiah was given a glimpse of God's glory and reflections of that experience permeate the next sixty chapters of the book bearing his name. Consider some things he wrote in light of now-known scientific fact (Isaiah 40:12, 26):

"Who has measured the waters in the hollow of His hand . . ." Physicists say the oceans alone comprise 130 million square miles of water, each square 13,000 feet deep! To the omnipotent God, this is less than a handful!

" . . . and marked off the heavens by the span . . ." From the Earth, we see

only one galaxy—the Milky Way, and it is 100,000 light-years in diameter. (A light-year is the distance light travels in a year at the rate of 300,000 kilometers per second.) This and some 50 billion other galaxies can be marked off by the span of the infinite God's hand.

" . . . *and calculated the dust of the earth by the measure . . .*" The weight (dust) of the earth is staggering—a six with twenty-one zeros after it, and every day some 80 million tons of cosmic dust are added to the universe! Yet to the immeasurable God, calculating this amount might be like our putting a spoon of sugar in our coffee.

"And see who has created these stars, the One who leads forth their host by number. He calls them all by name." In any one galaxy there are hundreds of millions of stars orbiting around a common center. The living God knows at every point exactly how many there are in the billions of galaxies, for He calls them by name.

This is only a taste of the greatness of the one true God. Surely He who holds this world together by His power is sufficient to satisfy the deepest longings of His own created children.

Created for Satisfaction in God

When Jesus stood up on the day before His arrest and cried out: "If any man is thirsty, let him come to me and drink" (John 7:37), it was a setup. He knew full well the condition of every soul there because He created them with a hunger and thirst for Him. God's plan from the beginning was to fashion a people for whom He would be the bread of life and the fountain that never runs dry. "For with you is the fountain of life; in your light we see light" (Psalm 36:9).

God promises to guide us, satisfying our desire in scorched places, making us like springs of water whose waters do not fail (Isaiah 58:11). How will He satisfy us? With himself! With His goodness: "I will fill the soul of the priests with abundance, and My people will be satisfied with My goodness" (Jeremiah 31:14). With His love: "O satisfy us in the morning with your lovingkindness, that we may sing for joy and be glad all our days" (Psalm 90:14). With His presence: "How blessed is the one whom you choose and bring near to you to dwell in your courts. We will be satisfied" (Psalm 65:4).

Saint Augustine described God's presence as "food that is not diminished by eating and an embrace that, no matter how satisfying, is never broken."[4] John of the Cross asked, "Is it any wonder that the soul feels it is being lifted and opened, rising as if on a current of pure and wordless joy, whenever He is near?"[5] From a Siberian labor camp, an imprisoned priest cried out in the aftermath of terrible torture: "There was but a single vision: God, who was all in all."[6] God created us to be satisfied in Him—we are hungry, we are thirsty, and He will ever, always be enough to fill us.

Ever Feeding on the Bread of Life

In ancient Persia, when an honored guest came to the palace to dine, they were to stand at the head of the table, where the king stuffed their mouths with candies and jewels. In like manner, our God calls each of us to the head of His banqueting table, saying, "Open your mouth wide and I will fill it" (Psalm 81:10).

Because God created us for His glory (Isaiah 43:7, 21), and because as John Piper says, "God is most glorified in us when we are most satisfied in Him,"[7] His very nature guarantees He will pour himself into us. The all-satisfying God of the Twenty-third Psalm promises we shall not want and invites us to dine with Him. He sets a beautiful table, replete with the cup of His kindness, the fruit of His faithfulness, the meat of His mercy, the bread of His justice, the produce of His patience, and the grapes of His goodness.

"But I would feed you with the finest of the wheat, and with honey from the rock I would satisfy you" (Psalm 81:16). When Jesus' body was broken on Calvary, He became the bread of life with which the Father would ever sustain our hungry hearts. When He was pleased to crush His only Son, sweet nectar burst forth—honey from the very Rock of our salvation. And one glorious day, the Lord God Omnipotent promises to serve us a lavish banquet, fully revealing His glory, wiping the tears from our eyes and swallowing death forever (Isaiah 25:6–9). From all eternity, God lives to quench our thirst and satisfy our souls with nothing less than himself.

Barriers to Contentment

When we feel restless, undone, and unfulfilled, we can rejoice, for that is how our faithful God calls us. Our lack is His gift to compel us to run to Him. If we don't respond to His call, the ache within will remain. The gods of our own making, though they may bring a short-lived reprieve, in the end cannot really help us. We can only keep searching hopelessly for a satisfaction that will never come. By not turning to God with our deepest desires, we face some tragic outcomes.

Disordered Desires

In the book *Hitler's Cross*, Erwin Lutzer traces the rise of the Third Reich by asking some haunting questions. Why did the German people, and more particularly the church, not part ways with Hitler once his real agenda became known? Though their initial deception might be understandable, why did they surrender their personal rights, enact laws that led to the extermination of eight million people, and favor a war that killed fifty million people in the greatest bloodbath in history?[8]

Though the reasons are complex and diverse, one thing is clear—they were a people whose cravings had gotten out of kilter, a people of disordered desire. This didn't happen overnight. Joblessness, poverty, national shame, and political corruption ran rampant, making the Germans prime targets for deception. Driven by the need for stability, security, and hope, they embraced Hitler as a savior who would deliver them from their misery.

Sadly, the Christian church looked no different from the rest of society. Hitler's successes enticed them as well, creating a sense of renewal within

their ranks. Glorying in the breadth of his dominion, their Führer ridiculed believers, saying, "Do you really believe the masses will be Christian again? Nonsense! Never again.... They will betray their God to us. They will betray anything for the sake of their miserable jobs and incomes."[9]

These words sound frighteningly like newspaper accounts of America in the waning months of the twentieth century. Where was the church in the face of grossly immoral national leadership? How many believers secretly wished the president's sexual escapades would fade into obscurity without threatening their retirement plans or well-established careers? Why did Christians not cry out en masse against a regime that sanctioned partial-birth abortion or a Congress that cut benefits to the poor while consistently fattening their own pork barrel legislation? Were we guilty of betraying our faith for job security or our savings accounts? Is the horror of the Holocaust so far removed that we can dismiss it as irrelevant to our own struggle?

Disordered desire is a dangerous thing, for it blinds our eyes to the depravity threatening to consume us. It causes us to run after other saviors, such as success, health, status, political security, or financial stability. These can end up being mirages in an empty stretch of wilderness, leaving us thirstier than before. God speaks keenly to the distress of disordered desire: "Why do you spend money for what is not bread, and your wages for what does not satisfy? Listen carefully to me, and eat what is good, and delight yourself in abundance. Incline your ear and come to me. Listen, that you may live" (Isaiah 55:2–3).

Why indeed? When we could delight in abundance, why do we expend our time, energy, and money day in and day out for that which only intensifies the void within? Why nibble the crumbs from the dustbin of deadly devotions when we could be feasting at the table of life?

Insatiable Desires

We are a nation of spenders, collectors, and possessors. We spend more than any country in the world—an average of ninety dollars per household every day. We spend $45 billion a year on entertainment and $21 billion on our pets. The waste we generate in one year alone would fill a convoy of ten-ton garbage trucks 145,000 miles long. As one newspaper editorial opined, "You really don't need all of this stuff, but you still want more. . . . Now it's not only your hobby, but a way of life."[10]

If we fail to find satisfaction in the living God, we will never be filled. The internal drive haunts us and our culture reinforces the lie that we must have more. In one evening of TV alone, two hundred and fifty messages tell us we're missing something. We have become a nation of gluttons, acting as if accumulation were an inalienable right of citizenship. One author wrote, "Insatiability itself is as old as humanity, or at least the fall of humanity. What is unique to modern consumerism is the idealization and constant encouragement of insatiability—the deification of dissatisfaction."[11]

Insatiability is the opposite of contentment, arising from the sad reality that what we have does not satisfy, and therefore we have no choice but to pursue more. The Israelites suffered this malady. Turning from the God who had so miraculously delivered and sustained them, they were filled with indefinable cravings. God gave them water, but they wanted bread. He gave them bread, and they wanted meat.

God gave them meat in ironic abundance—three feet of quail, a day's journey in every direction—so much that it made them sick. The psalmist writes of their continual dissatisfaction, noting that finally God brought their days to an end in complete futility (Psalm 78:33).

Paul tells us that this story is given for our instruction, to warn us against craving evil desires and putting God to the test (1 Corinthians 10:6). What can we learn from their example? If God isn't enough, nothing will ever satisfy. Like the Israelites choking on quail, we may be drowning in affluence, never realizing that though God has given us what we want, futility is our inevitable fate.

How this breaks the Father's heart. Can you hear His sorrow as He cries out, "What injustice did your fathers find in Me, that they went from Me

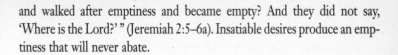

and walked after emptiness and became empty? And they did not say, 'Where is the Lord?' " (Jeremiah 2:5–6a). Insatiable desires produce an emptiness that will never abate.

Misdirected Desires

Sometimes the slip from the living God to a god of our own making is a subtle one. Perhaps we've tasted the joy of knowing Him, but our focus has slowly shifted to other things—usually good things. These can be the Sunday school class we teach or the children we raise. It may be goals for our future or the work we do each day. Because these are worthwhile endeavors, they can be quite dangerous, for they satisfy for a season.

In my early years of writing I experienced this. God had made it clear that writing was His will for my life, but soon I became enthralled with the idea of being a published author. Before I knew it, I was consumed with writing *for* God instead of living to hear His voice. When I didn't succeed as I thought I should, I complained to God about why He wasn't blessing me. His Spirit stirred my heart with questions: *What if you are to write only for Me? What if you never get published? What if I am taking you through this process simply so you can know Me more and glorify Me in the quietness of your own home?*

As I pondered these questions through the coming days, I realized how my focus had shifted. Though my heart was once pure, my desire for God had turned into a drive to write, albeit in His name. Good desires, even God-given desires, can be misdirected. This is Satan's insidious plan to keep us from passionate intimacy with Christ. The Evil One loves to see us working hard, busy for the kingdom at a frantic pace, as long as we don't experience the wonder of resting completely in the sufficiency of almighty God, joyfully drinking from the well of His salvation.

The church at Ephesus was duped by misdirected desire. They were an example of purity and devotion by anyone's standards. They worked hard, persevered through trials, tested their leaders, and rejected evil, all for

Christ's name. But God's message to them was heartbreaking: "I have this against you, that you have left your first love" (Revelation 2:4).

When anything but a love affair with our Creator consumes and spurs us on, disappointment and disillusionment are not far behind. Burned out and weary, we question God. *This isn't fair. I'm tired—can't someone else do this ministry for a while? What are you doing? When will you answer my prayers? Why did you ever call me to this?*

The answer is simple. God doesn't call us to a career, a ministry, or even a lifestyle. He doesn't call us primarily to be mothers or fathers, preachers or engineers, missionaries or layleaders, musicians or writers. First and foremost, God calls us to himself, to be His own. "For in Him we live and move and exist. . . . For we also are His children" (Acts 17:28). God and God alone is our reason for being, and He alone can fill our emptiness. When we live in the truth of this, everything else will fall into place in a wonderful joy-filled rhythm of life empowered by God's Spirit.

What We Must Do

One of the greatest deficiencies of the church today is in connecting with God on what the saints of old called an experimental level. Though we possess vast quantities of information concerning the God we serve, much of it never moves from our heads to our hearts. As Martin Lloyd-Jones so poignantly asked, "Is not this our trouble, my dear friends, that we talk about God and we believe in God but do we know God, the glory of God?"[12]

Since God operates in the spiritual realm (known in His Word as "the heavenlies"), we desperately need the eyes of our heart enlightened so that we might really see what is before us. Thus, in many ways, finding contentment is not about doing something, but seeing Someone.

Cry Out for a Fresh Revelation

The theme of spiritual blindness is ubiquitous in Scripture, warning us often to understand our real need. David proclaimed that only the Lord could "open the eyes of the blind" (Psalm 146:8). Isaiah confirmed that God would lead the *blind by a way they do not know, in paths they do not know* (Isaiah 42:16). Jesus came with the promise that He would *open blind eyes* (Isaiah 42:7) and told the Pharisees that they were the blind leading the blind because though their outward behavior was impeccable, their hearts were far from Him (Matthew 15:14; 23:26).

This is why Paul prayed that God would grant the church a "spirit of wisdom and revelation in the knowledge of Him" (Ephesians 1:17). We must understand that our most glaring need is for a fresh revelation of God and of what He sees when He looks at our hearts.

"Be appalled, O heavens, at this, and shudder, be very desolate." Surely these must be some of the most sobering words in all of Scripture. Jehovah God calls the sun, moon, stars, planets, galaxies, and perhaps legions of angels to join Him in utter dismay. What elicits such a response? What so appalls the Almighty? At what horror does He shudder to the point of desolation? "For My people have committed two evils: they have forsaken Me, the fountain of living waters, to hew for themselves cisterns, broken cisterns that can hold no water" (Jeremiah 2:12–13).

Surely something that so appalls God must give us pause, if not stop us dead in our tracks. If God calls the heavens to shudder, dare we ignore such a lament? What are these evils He is desolate over? Broken cisterns are the idols of the heart we have fashioned to feed our starving souls. They are spiritually life-threatening. Through the discontent that plagues us, at times God beckons, sometimes gently tapping and other times pounding on the door of our hearts that we might let Him have His rightful place.

After telling the church at Laodicea how He felt about their lack of passion for Him, God implored them to understand their true condition. "Because you say, 'I am rich, and have become wealthy, and have need of nothing,' and you do not know that you are wretched and miserable and poor and blind and naked. . . . Those whom I love, I reprove and discipline; therefore be zealous and repent" (Revelation 3:17, 19).

We are desperately needy and may not even know it. When broken cisterns have become our refuge, we are in bondage and the only way out is repentance before God. How do we repent if we are blinded to our need? This will require something far deeper than agreeing with God that we've sinned, quoting 1 John 1:9, and going on our way.

Our only hope for true repentance is to see God as He is and ourselves in light of His glory. We must continually cry out for divine revelation of our true condition, for this is the only thing that can change us. Isaiah saw God and was undone, Job covered his mouth, Daniel lost all his strength, Paul called Christ "unspeakable," and John fell as if dead. Nothing but a manifestation of the living God will uproot us from the hardened soil of hearts that cannot see.

We need to come to the Word and plead with God to disclose himself to us as He did there. He is a consuming fire, so we ask Him to inflame all the pieces of our lives with His presence. He demands that people tremble in His presence, so we ask Him to shake us until we do. He is a zealous lover, so we ask Him to break our hearts by showing us the way we've rebuffed His tender advances.

We must not cease to cry out until the rivers of God's glory begin to flow, causing us to flee with disgust those things that once held sway over our lives. Until we feel about our apostasy as God does, we will never take the bold action to renounce the idols we've served. Without spiritual revelation, our houses and cars and lands and clothes and vacations and toys and careers will continue to provide a pseudo-satisfaction that brings not life, but death and destruction, dishonoring the God we say we love.

Drink From the Well of Salvation

When digging for an underground stream, workers often have to bore through beds of sandy soil, even breaking up rocky layers. But if they dig deep enough, they find clear, cool, refreshing springwater. It's the same in our lives. We have to burrow through our busyness, our plans and purposes,

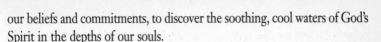

our beliefs and commitments, to discover the soothing, cool waters of God's Spirit in the depths of our souls.

Often we must make radical choices to stop drinking from the wells of this world. In our culture of "muchness and manyness,"[13] dozens of things fill every waking moment. By pulling away from some of these, we may discover what we've been running to for sustenance and how these might be a broken cistern, replacing the presence of God.

I believe we would be astonished if we knew how many times a day God calls our name. He showed me this several months ago when health problems required me to eliminate all types of sugar from my diet. I was completely unprepared for the battle that ensued. Because I'd never been greatly overweight, I didn't think food was an issue in my spiritual life. I was wrong. In the first several weeks I found myself irritable, frustrated, depressed, and wanting to avoid social contact.

Fixated on food several times a day, I wondered why I felt such emptiness. After a long barren stretch, God spoke, telling me that for years He'd been calling me to himself, but instead I'd continued to lap water from the gutter of a fallen world. Though He'd tried to reveal this many times, I'd always dismissed His gentle voice, thinking it too silly a notion that a cookie could replace Christ in my affections.

What might be the broken cisterns you run to? With what are you feeding your soul? It could be listening to the radio in the car or watching TV in the evenings. It might be shopping for clothes, ministering in your church, or volunteering in your community. It could be sports leagues, or working long hours, or your children's extracurricular activities, or eating junk food, or just plain busyness.

Whatever it might be, determine for a time to give it up. Instead of rushing to fill the empty space, listen to the still, small voice of our Lord. This is one of the great joys of fasting. When we go without food or entertainment or any number of things, we discover what has really consumed us and how God can fill every empty spot in our soul. But we must take the time to wait, to rest, to be still, and become completely empty. If we fill the void ourselves it will be temporary and vacuous at best, and we'll miss the over-flowing and refreshing water of the Spirit, who lives to sustain us.

Feed on God Continually

Years ago as missionaries in the Alaskan bush, we got our water from a pump. To make it work, we put a little water in the top, then pumped the handle vigorously about thirty-five times. When the water finally gushed out, we filled buckets to last a few days. Having been raised in the city, we didn't know the secret of a primed pump until an Eskimo explained it to us.

It was so simple. If we pumped water *every* day, it was always at the top, ready to pour out at the first crank. If we let it go more than one day, how-ever, we had to go through the entire ritual of priming and pumping once again.

Our spiritual lives can look a lot like that. We attend church or Bible study or some conference, and *pump, pump, pump* until we experience the flow of living water. Then we get caught up in our busy lives until the next week when we *pump, pump, pump* all over again. God never intended it to be this way. Mother Teresa wrote,

> Never give up this daily intimate contact with Jesus as the real living person—not just the idea. How can we last even one day with-out hearing Jesus say, 'I love you'? Impossible. Our soul needs that as much as the body needs air to breathe. If not, prayer is dead—meditation, only thinking. Jesus wants you each to hear Him—speaking in the silence of your heart.[14]

God calls us to come to Him continually—in moments alone with Him every day, and then throughout the day, discovering the wonderful secret that when we do, refreshment is right there, ready to be enjoyed.

Get Greedy for God

Those who experience the thrill of satisfaction in God can never settle for the ordinary again. The waters this world offers are a bitter taste in their mouths as they reclaim their birthright of joy and peace in the Holy Spirit. Why, then, would anyone resist? What could we possibly fear? Fenelon prayed four hundred years ago: "But how is it, O my divine bridegroom, that we fear to break our chains? Do passing vanities mean more than Thy eternal truth and Thou Thyself? Can we fear to give ourselves to thee? O monstrous folly! That would be to fear for our happiness."[15]

How our lives would change if we were greedy for God, praying every morning: "Lord, you blessed me yesterday in a thousand ways, but I need more. I didn't get enough of you—I want to see your face in all things, inhabit your love every moment, ride on your pinions across the expanse of my busyness, tremble in awe at your mighty roar—God, I want more, more, more, more, more!"

God relishes these kinds of prayers, in fact, dares us to pray them. Consider some of His brazen claims:

"Call to Me and I will answer you, and I will tell you great and mighty things, which you do not know" (Jeremiah 33:3).

"The Lord is near to all who call upon Him, to all who call upon Him in truth. He will fulfill the desire of those who fear Him; He will also hear their cry and will save them" (Psalm 145:18–19).

"So I say to you, ask, and it will be given to you; seek, and you will find; knock, and it will be opened to you. For everyone who asks, receives; and he who seeks, finds; and to him who knocks, it will be opened" (Luke 11:9–10).

"For . . . the same Lord is Lord of all, abounding in riches for all who call on Him" (Romans 10:12).

"Now to Him who is able to do far more abundantly beyond all that we ask or think, according to the power that works within us, to Him be the glory" (Ephesians 3:20–21).

How God longs to pour out blessings on those who will find their satisfaction in Him. It is His idea—He ever lives to fill us up. Why wouldn't we come and drink?

The Ocean of God's Glory

In an article in *USA Today* entitled "By the sea, by the sea, how happy we'll be without a pool," the author surmised that the world is divided into two groups—pool people and ocean people. Having spent most of my life near the ocean, I readily related to his humorous anecdotes. He noted the absurdity of Americans building swimming pools right on the ocean's edge, thinking we can do better than nature by painting it turquoise. Reminiscing over his childhood, he told how a rectangle of water in the middle of a parking lot wowed him the first time he left the farm and stayed at a Holiday Inn. Then he mused:

> But after I saw the ocean, the Holiday Inn pool seemed, well, inadequate. I ask you, can you take a long walk along a pool? Can you pick up wonderful things around a pool, take them home, keep them forever? Can your dog romp for miles along a pool? Can you sit and gaze out at a pool for hours on end? Can a pool outside your window lull you to sleep?
>
> Pool people, of course, say the ocean is messy. There are things in there, they cry! And waves that knock you down! And all that sand in your bathing suit!
>
> Well, that's the whole point. It's noisy and bawdy and unpredictable and gives off a glorious smell when irritated. And sometimes it's just downright rude. It throws sand in your face. That's the fun of it. The ocean makes you laugh. A pool never does.[16]

As I reflected on his words that day, it occurred to me that there are two kinds of people in the church as well. There are those who are not experiencing the living God and instead serve a lesser god of their own making.

Like pool people they build a life, paint it with religious activity and good works, and fill it with the wealth of this world. They keep it clean, manage it well, and believe this is the best they can hope for. Tragically, just beyond the edge of their existence lies the ocean of God's glory.

And oh, what an ocean it is! There have always been those eager to ride its waves, explore its depths, and be continually confounded by its power. True, they've learned it can be a messy place. El Shaddai knocks them down and throws sand in their faces. The Lion of Judah is unpredictable. He roars and reacts magnificently when irritated. But oh, how the King of Glory makes us laugh. His face shines into our soul, creating a bubbling cauldron of joy that seeps up and out of the depths of our being. Life without that, no matter how we embellish it, is only a caricature of the real thing. All the while the extraordinary ocean of God's glory beckons to every one of us. How could we ever resist?

TAKING UP OUR CROSS—
What We Gain and What We Lose

Taking up our cross against discontent simply means to recognize the things we have turned to or the god we have created in response to our hunger for the living God. Reckoning ourselves dead to these things through the power of His Spirit, we experience incredible gains. Hope begins to seep through our being like water to a barren land. The futility of a fallen world dissipates in light of His plans for our life.

Gain Hope

" 'For I know the plans that I have for you,' declares the Lord, 'plans for welfare and not for calamity to give you a future and a *hope*. Then you will call upon Me and come and pray to Me, and I will listen to you. You will seek Me and find Me when you search for Me with all your heart' " (Jeremiah 29:11–13).

Lose Futility

"You must not turn aside, for then you would go after *futile* things which can not profit or deliver, because they are *futile*. For the Lord will not abandon His people on account of His great name, because the Lord has been pleased to make you a people for Himself" (1 Samuel 12:21–22).

Instead of buying the lie that we don't have enough, we find ourselves enthralled with the mystery of what we do have. Filled with the joy of knowing our Lord, our lips cease grumbling and complaining, causing us to stand out like lights against the stormy backdrop of an unhappy world.

Gain Joy

"You will make known to me the path of life; in your presence is fullness of *joy*; in your right hand there are pleasures forever" (Psalm 16:11).

"For you make him blessed forever; you make him *joyful* with gladness in your presence" (Psalm 21:6).

Lose Grumbling and Complaining

"Do all things without *grumbling* or *disputing*; so that you will prove yourselves to be blameless and innocent, children of God, above reproach in the midst of a crooked and perverse generation, among whom you appear as lights in the world" (Philippians 2:14–15).

Seeking fulfillment in anything other than God is a destructive endeavor. Eventually our dreams of success become nightmares that haunt us with the truth that we are empty. But as we die to the deceit of worldly allurements and live unto God, we enjoy a satisfaction that no person or situation can ever take from us.

Gain Satisfaction

"As for me, I shall behold your face in righteousness; I will be *satisfied* with your likeness when I awake" (Psalm 17:15).

"For He has *satisfied* the thirsty soul, and the hungry soul He has filled with what is good" (Psalm 107:9).

Lose Dissatisfaction

"They will fling their silver into the streets and their gold will become an abhorrent thing; their silver and their gold will not be able to deliver them in the day of the wrath of the Lord. They *cannot satisfy* their appetite nor can they fill their stomachs" (Ezekiel 7:19).

When eternity with Christ consumes our thoughts and plans, we are no longer bound by the belief systems of this world. We stand aloof from their trickery, fully aware that our life here is a vapor. The reality of our eternal destiny frees us from the devastation of clinging to all that is being corrupted before our very eyes.

Gain Freedom

"For speaking out arrogant words of vanity they entice by fleshly desires, by sensuality, those who barely escape from the ones who live in error, promising them freedom while they themselves are slaves of corruption; for by what a man is overcome, by this he is enslaved" (2 Peter 2:18–19).

Lose Bondage

"But those who want to get rich fall into temptation and a *snare* and many foolish and harmful desires which plunge men into ruin and destruction" (1 Timothy 6:9).

"Be on guard, so that your hearts will not be weighted down with ... the worries of life, and that day will not come on you suddenly like a *trap*" (Luke 21:34).

Nothing is more tiring and less fulfilling than self-reliance. At some point we come to the end of our natural strength, and there is literally nowhere else to turn. But when we make God our delight, we learn to rest in His sufficiency. Only then can we live out the supernatural paradox of strength made great in weakness.

Gain Spiritual Strength

"And He has said to me, 'My grace is sufficient for you, for power is perfected in weakness.' Mostly gladly, therefore I will rather boast about my weaknesses, so that the power of Christ may dwell in me. Therefore I am well content with weaknesses, with insults, with distresses, with persecutions, with difficulties, for Christ's sake; for when I am weak, then I am *strong*" (2 Corinthians 12:9–10).

Lose Self-Reliance

"Woe to those who go down to Egypt for help and rely on horses and trust in chariots because they are many and in horsemen because they are very strong, but they do not look to the Holy One of Israel, nor seek the Lord! . . . their horses are *flesh and not spirit*; so the Lord will stretch out His hand, and he who helps will stumble and who is helped will fall, and all of them will come to an end together" (Isaiah 31:1–3).

This is only a taste of what contentment brings to the soul. Who wouldn't want to die to destructive deeds of the flesh such as futility, grumbling, and complaining; dissatisfaction, bondage, and self-reliance? Oh, what treasure awaits those who willingly follow Jesus to His crucifixion. For the hope, joy, satisfaction, freedom, and spiritual strength set before us, we readily endure the cross.

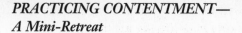

PRACTICING CONTENTMENT—
A Mini-Retreat

Because Satan (the prince of this world) is the great deceiver, and since the lusts of our flesh are very strong, it is easy to be trusting in broken cisterns, serving a god of our own making, all the while starving on a spiritual level. This extended season of prayer and reflection will help you get in touch with what actually does fill your life and what steps you can take to enter into the contentment of a satisfied soul.

Preparing Your Heart

Take a few minutes to quiet your mind before the Lord. Acknowledge His presence with words from your heart or a prayer such as the following:

> *Lord, you are here. I welcome you and open myself to your gentle presence. I thank you that I do not have to find you, for you have already found me. I rest in this. Praising your glorious and precious name, I invite you to reveal yourself to me today in new and fresh ways. I need you. Make yourself at home in our time together.*

Read Psalm 104 slowly and with feeling to the Lord. (You may want to personalize all the verses by putting "You" in place of "He.") Pause as His Spirit nudges you to contemplate the words you read. Reflect on His uncommon greatness.

Now read Isaiah 55:1–2 and John 7:37–39. Write a prayer of expectation to the Lord based on these verses.

Contemplating His Presence

People dying of thirst in the desert are often fooled by the presence of a mirage. They see water in the distance and exert all their energy to get to it, their strong thirst driving them to that which looks like the answer to their need. Instead, they end up in a barren place, thirst unquenched, Death knocking at their door.

But sometimes in the middle of the desert, places of refreshment can be found. These uncharacteristic green spots are called oases. Because of the water there, they represent a refuge from the dry, infertile wasteland. Unfortunately, many who might quench their thirst in them have exhausted their energy chasing mirages that could not satisfy, and when the real oasis appears, they have stopped short, spent and weary from their dismal journey.

Ask God to show you what things you run to for satisfaction, the mirages you chase—whether it be food, fun, busyness, ministry, sports, TV, books—anything that might be luring you away from His refreshing presence. When you have finished, read the following paragraphs a couple of times. Then close your eyes and allow yourself to experience this as if it were happening to you at this moment.

> *The day is unbearably hot, the journey a weary one. Feeling the heat like a weight against your body, you long for something to drink—just a little water to quench your thirst and soothe your dry throat. As far as your eye can see, though, there is nothing but hot, barren sand. How much farther before you will find help?*
>
> *Dropping to one knee in exhaustion, something flashes ahead of you. There, just a short distance away, you see it—the glimmer of water. Feeling your heart begin to pound, you find renewed energy. Rising, you begin to run toward it. Finally . . . But the strangest thing happens as you draw near. The beautiful pond disappears and in its place you see only more sand. Disillusioned, all you can do is strike out again, hope diminishing as you go.*
>
> *Slowly, sweat dripping from your pores, you move on. The fear grows inside you:* What if I never find the end of this desert? What if there is no water and I die here? *Desperation clutches your heart like a vise. You begin to move faster, though your legs feel like lead. There—there it is! Far off in the distance is a grand lake—sparkling, bubbling with life. If*

only you can get to it. Now you run with all your might, closing your eyes against the battering wind of the desert.

Running . . . running . . . running. . . . Then falling on your face in exhaustion, you taste the gritty sand. Mustering up strength you raise your eyes to see how far you still have to go. But there is nothing there—only empty miles of sand—nothing to quench the terrible thirst that threatens to undo you.

Now you know there is no hope and all is an illusion meant to kill what life you have left. Why bother going on? Sinking down again, you gulp for a breath of air, but the dryness fills your throat and it seems as if your lungs are on fire.

Facedown, spent and undone, you hear a voice: "Is anyone thirsty?"

You lie there, very, very still, and you hear it again. "Is anyone thirsty?" Raising your head slightly, you hear it again, and this time it calls your name, " _____ , are you thirsty?"

"Yes, yes," your heart cries out as you struggle to your feet. That voice— it is so strong and compelling—almost hypnotic, calling you forth. It's as if you can do nothing but turn toward it. Aching to hear it again, you look around, anguish now laced with hope. There it is again. "If anyone is thirsty, let him come to me and drink."

Drawing to your feet, you turn toward the voice that has drawn closer and closer. When you look up, you see Him. It is the Lord—the friend of sinners—Jesus the Christ. Holding out His hands to you, He speaks with overwhelming gentleness and yet great force:

"If anyone is thirsty, come to me and drink. For as Scripture says, if you believe in Me, out of your being will flow rivers of living water."

With what strength you have left, you move toward Him, falling at His feet in exhaustion. Then you feel it—a sprinkle on your neck. Cool, cool water raining down . . . down . . . down. Now in a rush it pours over you, drenching you with freshness and life.

Turning your face upward, you open your mouth and let the water run in until it infuses every part of your being. In this moment you know that nothing has ever or will ever taste this good. This is where you are meant to be . . . this is the well that never runs dry, that never ceases to flood forth with living water. Nothing else will ever do. This you know as deeply as anything you've ever known in your life.

Responding to His Call

Read John 4:9–14. See yourself as the one trying to give Jesus what you have, not realizing who He is. Listen carefully to His words to you. Meditate on them for a few minutes—put your name in the blank and hear Him speak:

"_____, if you knew the gift of God, and *who* it is who says to you, 'Give Me a drink,' you would have asked Him, and He would have given you living water."

In quietness before the living God, ask Him to do two things:

First, to open your eyes to *who* it is that offers you this living water.

Second, to give you to drink from the well of His eternal fountain.

Spend as much time as you need to allow Him to do this work. Write a response in your prayer journal.

End your time with thanksgiving based on the following verses. You may want to write them into a prayer: Psalm 36:7–9; 90:14; 73:24–25, 28.

Going Forward

It is an amazing thing that God ever lives to fill us with himself. The contentment that comes from feasting on Him is beyond imagination. When we experience it, we live in a state of awe at His goodness and love. We know we have nothing to give in light of all He's given. Trembling, we see how we stumble, falter, sin, and fail, and yet He is there. This is the start of a crushing through which seeds of humility are planted in our heart. Let us go on to pursue this precious virtue.

Notes

1. R. C. Sproul, *The Soul's Quest for God* (Wheaton, Ill.: Tyndale House Publishers, 1992), ix.

2. Charles Colson, "Les Misérables: The Culture of Discontent," *Breakpoint*, February 9, 1996, http://www.breakpoint.org/scripts/60209.htm.

3. A. W. Tozer, *The Knowledge of the Holy* (New York: Harper & Row, 1961), vii-viii.

4. Augustine of Hippo, *Augustine's Confessions* (Grand Rapids, Mich.: Sovereign Grace Publishers, 1971), 189.

5. Arranged and paraphrased by David Hazard, *You Set My Spirit Free: A 40-Day Journey in the Company of John of the Cross* (Minneapolis: Bethany House Publishers, 1994), 139.

6. Father Walter Ciszek, *He Leadeth Me* (San Francisco: Ignatius Press, 1973), 79.

7. John Piper, *Desiring God: Meditations of a Christian Hedonist* (Portland, Ore.: Multnomah Press, 1996), 97.

8. Erwin Lutzer, *Hitler's Cross* (Chicago: Moody Press, 1995), 18.

9. Waite, *Adolf Hitler: The Psychopathic God* (New York: Basic Books, 1968), 16.

10. Clark Morphew, "People Living a Life of Scant Materialism Find It Simply Rewarding," *San Diego Union Tribune*, August 7, 1998.

11. Rodney Clapp, "Does the Devil Take Visa?" *Christianity Today* (Oct. 7, 1996): 40:2.

12. Martin Lloyd-Jones, *Joy Unspeakable* (Wheaton, Ill.: Harold Shaw Publishers, 1984), 87.

13. Richard Foster, *Prayer: Finding the Heart's True Home* (Harper San Francisco, 1992), 1.

14. Mother Teresa of Calcutta, *Works of Love Are Works of Peace: A Photographic Record by Michael Collopy* (San Francisco: Ignatius Press, 1996), 197.

15. Francois Fenelon, *Christian Perfection* (New York: Harper & Row, 1947), 74.

16. Craig Lewis, "The Final Word," *USA Today*, July 16, 1998.

CHAPTER FOUR
HUMILITY

If you should ask me what are the ways of God, I would tell you that the first is humility, the second is humility, and the third is still humility. Not that there are no other precepts to give, but if humility does not precede all that we do, our efforts are fruitless.[1]

Saint Augustine

I have started this chapter at least a dozen times. I've walked away, deleted page after page, cried, and asked God to release me from writing it. The nature of the subject has weighed heavily upon me. It seems that every time I get close to finishing, God reveals more sin in my life. Like Pandora's box that won't close, pride keeps popping up.

How do you write about something of which you know so little? How do you inspire when your own journey is more about failure than success, insecurity than confidence, and weakness than strength? This has been my struggle.

Early in my Christian walk, pride was blatant—I was easily offended, often defensive, and relished being the center of attention. When God began to reveal these things to me, I determined to change. I learned to hold my tongue, dodge conflict, and avoid demanding the spotlight.

After a while God did a deeper work, showing me pride in my thought life. I saw that though I didn't speak or act upon it, my heart was still filled with jealousy, envy, petty criticism, and self-centeredness. Once again, I committed myself to change.

Then something happened that peeled layers of flesh from my heart, leaving me raw before the Lord. I was speaking at a retreat that had been a struggle from the earliest planning stages. Because I had felt so strongly led of God to go, I thanked Him in advance for the opportunity to "humble myself" in the face of the group's disorganization and seeming lack of concern for me.

I was humbled, but not in the way I expected. Early the first morning some words of a song playing in the background startled me out of a prayerful reverie: "It's all about You, Jesus . . . and all this is for You, for Your glory and Your fame. . . . It's not about me, as if You should do things my way. . . . You alone are God and I surrender to Your ways."[2]

With painful clarity, I grasped that humility wasn't about what I thought or did or how I acted or spoke. Humility wasn't about me at all. To be humble meant to be so caught up in Jesus and so zealous for His glory that all thought of self vanished. To be humble meant to live every moment in keen awareness that it is all, always, all about Him.

I understood then that my past notions of humility required actions that anyone could learn. But the humility God was revealing could never be achieved by trying, diligent though I might be. In my best efforts to keep Christ central, thoughts of self would always creep in unannounced, polluting me with pride. In my entire spiritual life I had never felt more helpless.

And still I struggle. "Will we ever be humble?" I asked my husband as I determined to write of this elusive virtue.

His answer revealed volumes: "The longer I live, the more I realize that I will always be more ignorant than knowledgeable, more in bondage than free, more blind than I can see, and more proud than humble. For me, this has been distressing at times, but also terribly freeing."

Distressing? Yes, for like the apostle Paul, we find ourselves overwhelmed at our inadequacy, crying out, "Wretched man that I am, who will set me free from this body of death?" But through the wall of our unworthiness, the answer rings: "Thanks be to God, through Jesus Christ our

Lord!" (Romans 7:24–25). Christ is our answer—He is our adequacy, our sufficiency, our worthiness, and our hope. And when we come to the end of ourselves, unable to run anywhere but into His arms, awestruck by the mystery of grace, we know we are free.

HUMILITY

Living in the wonder of the extravagant grace that
God pours out in exchange for my inadequacy.

The spiritual journey is a paradox. Pride compels us to work harder and do better, while humility rests in the reality that we'll never get it perfect. Pride makes us believe life is about winning, while humility takes comfort in the inevitability of defeat. I am trying to learn to live in this strange dichotomy; helpless yet rejoicing that I can cry out to Christ and He will do what He has promised from the beginning—live His life through my earthen vessel. This is both the foundation and the fruit of a humble life.

Foundations for Humility

Humility was the most distinguishing mark of Jesus our Lord. He humbled Himself to the extreme—the point of death (Philippians 2:7). How can we ever expect to become like Him, empowered to imitate His sacrificial existence (Ephesians 5:1)? Since we know we could never aspire to that kind of profound humility, our hope must be in what God will do in and through us. The key is in learning how we in our weakness can draw from His infinite strength. Some of the most powerful truths we must see are that God has need of nothing, He is always the Giver, and we are in desperate need of His grace.

God Has Need of Nothing

The wonder that Christ has chosen us and made us His own can't help but elicit profound gratitude from our deepest being. Our natural response is to want to show our appreciation, to pay Him back for what He's done. David experienced this when God made him king and all his country was finally at peace. Feeling deeply thankful, he called Nathan the prophet to tell him it just didn't seem right to have a beautiful home, while the Ark of the Covenant still stood in a tent. Nathan immediately got the picture, telling David to go ahead and build a dwelling for the ark, for God was with him.

But God did not approve. Waking Nathan up in the middle of the night, He spoke: "Go and say to My servant David, 'Thus says the Lord, "Are you the one who should build Me a house to dwell in? Wherever I have gone with all the sons of Israel, did I speak a word . . . saying, 'Why have you not built Me a house of cedar?'"'" (2 Samuel 7:5, 7). Although God's goodness can't help but cause us to be grateful, He makes it abundantly clear we have no payback to give Him.

God's giving and ours are so very different. When we give a birthday gift, we take for granted that the favor will be returned on our birthday. When we accept a dinner invitation, we make a mental check to have them to our house as well. Our subconscious assumption is that God works like we do and therefore must expect us to do something to return the favor of saving our souls. But He doesn't.

It comes as a great shock to many that God simply does not need us and is not waiting in heaven for us to "work till Jesus comes" in order to pay Him off. God told the Israelites He needed nothing from them because everything was His in the first place: "If I were hungry I would not tell you, for the world is Mine, and all it contains" (Psalm 50:12).

Recently I challenged a group of pastors' wives to consider the question, "If God doesn't need me, then why do I do what I do?" Every one of us needs to grapple with this issue or we will live in the prideful bondage of thinking our efforts somehow become installments on the eternal debt incurred by our sin. We do owe Christ an incredible debt but it is one we could never repay. This is why He offers it as a free gift.

Since God is complete in His manifold perfections, He needs nothing. "Are you the one to build a house for me?" He challenged David. Paul understood this, saying, "The God who made the world and all things in it, since He is Lord of heaven and earth, does not dwell in temples made with hands, nor is He served by human hands, *as though He needed anything*, since he Himself gives to all people life and breath and all things" (Acts 17:24–25). This reality must begin to permeate our thinking if we want to experience the depths of grace God has poured out upon us.

God Is Always the Giver

After God made it clear to Nathan that David should not even try to repay Him for His blessings, He completely turned the tables, declaring instead what He was going to do on his behalf: "I will make you a great name.... I will give you rest from all your enemies. The Lord ... will make a house for you.... I will raise up your descendant ... and I will establish his kingdom.... I will be a father to him and he will be a son to Me.... Your house and your kingdom shall endure before Me forever; your throne shall be established forever"(2 Samuel 7:9–16, selected).

God's passion to give stems from the core of His being. He is a sun and a shield, giving grace and glory, withholding no good thing from those who walk uprightly (Psalm 84:11). God's giving is unlike anything we can humanly imagine for it is *charis* giving, or *grace* giving—freely bestowed on all who would receive it. He lavishes riches upon us from the infinite treasury of His glory.

There is a subtle misunderstanding often taught in spiritual circles that actually diminishes the greatness of our God. We hear it in statements like "She really sacrificed her life for God" or "God deserves my very best." We are being presumptuous, acting as if we have something we did not receive, when we think God is enriched by the things we do, the money we give, the ministry we are involved in, or the sacrificial choices we make. It would be like a beggar on the street trying to give you fifty cents to say thanks for the twenty you just gave him. He is the one in need but acts as if he has something to give, when all he has is what you've given him.

God is always the Giver, and we are always the receivers. Everything we have or are has come from His hand to us. More than that, He is continually increasing His benefits toward us. Truly, you cannot beat God in giving. David wanted to build an earthly house for God, but instead God gave *him* a house, and what a house it was! Hundreds of years later from the house of David came the "horn of salvation," Jesus Christ (Luke 1:69). Our redemption is a living declaration of God's propensity to give freely and without reserve. "He who did not spare His own Son, but delivered Him over for us all, how will He not also with Him freely give us all things?" (Romans 8:32).

God's Grace Is My Greatest Need

In his famous nineteenth-century work *The Hound of Heaven*, Francis Thompson poignantly depicts life's painful search for happiness. Running here and there, clinging to elusive joy and transient peace, avoiding inevitable confrontation with our own emptiness, we press on. But always at our heels is the relentless God, shining His grace through the dark caverns of our desperate soul. Thompson's poem, often thought autobiographical, eloquently describes God's words to him at the end of his barren quest:

How dost thou merit—
Of all man's clotted clay the dingiest clot?
Alack, thou knowest not
How little worthy of any love thou art!
Whom wilt thou find to love ignoble thee,
Save Me, save only Me?

"The dingiest clot of all man's clotted clay" is surely not a pretty picture. Yet God's Word tells us our hearts are wicked and deceitful, and our most righteous works are like filthy rags in His sight. On our own we were separated from Christ, excluded from His family, strangers to His ways, without God, and having no hope in this world (Ephesians 2:12). As hard as we may work to earn the approval and love of others, God sees through our bravado, and in His eyes we are always weak and needy creatures.

What we think we must accomplish tends to loom large in our own vision, causing us to sense a great weight about our time on this earth. But Scripture tells us we are a vapor, a breath, and barely a shadow in light of eternity. To almighty God, all the nations are like a speck of dust on a scale, so our existence is surely a miniscule one (Isaiah 40:15). We come into the world with nothing of our own and will leave it the same way (Job 1:21).

Paul proclaimed: "By the grace of God I am what I am" (1 Corinthians 15:10). Every breath we take affirms our complete dependence on an infinite and Sovereign Being. That He takes thought of us is deeply moving; that He blesses us is awe-inspiring. David was so overwhelmed that God desired nothing from him, wanting to bless him instead, that he exclaimed, "Who am I, O Lord God, and what is my house, that You have brought me this far? And yet this was insignificant in Your eyes, O Lord God. . . . What more can David say to You? For this reason you are great, O Lord God, for there is none like You, and there is no God besides You"(2 Samuel 7:18, 22).

Truly, there is no one like our God. Nowhere do we more clearly apprehend this than when His magnificent greatness and our complete inadequacy collide in the Cross of Christ. We come to Calvary with nothing in our hands but the sin that would bind our souls to an eternity in hell. Placing our depravity upon Christ's shoulders, we receive the gracious gift of atonement, seeing once and for all that everything we have, or are, or ever will be comes from Him. We can only cry out, "Who am I that you have brought me this far?"

Barriers to Humility

In light of these truths, it would seem easy to be humble. So where does the battle lie? Much of it is rooted in misunderstanding concerning our walk with God. We affirm our inadequacy but believe we must do something about it before God can use us. Knowing we are saved by grace, we tend to live as if we are sanctified—made righteous—through our own efforts. But true humility knows the immense relief of laying down every attempt to be good enough, work hard enough, produce fruit enough, grow fast enough, or please God enough. Identifying these is perhaps the first step to embracing the incredible wonder of grace.

We Lay Down Our Works

Like the Pharisees of Jesus' day, our belief that we must come to God from a position of strength causes us to impose external standards of spirituality on others and ourselves. The rules vary from church to church and age to age, but the underlying assumption is the same: God can most greatly use us when we get it right and do what we're supposed to do. My parents, therefore, would never miss a meeting at church, a criterion for godliness continually reinforced from the pulpit. The ritual of daily quiet times measured in weekly accountability groups was my entrée into the elite club of *good Christians.* Day after day believers labor in vain, working for God in ways He never intended.

There is great comfort in seeing that Jesus demonstrated not self-reliant diligence but dependency on the Father as a way of life. He chastised the Pharisees for their religious zeal and perplexed His followers with startling confessions of neediness. "The Son can do nothing of Himself. . . . I can do nothing on My own initiative . . . the words I say to you I do not speak on My own. . . . I have not even come on My own, but He sent Me. . . . Apart from Me you can do nothing" (John 5:19,30; 8:28; 14:10; 8:42; 15:5).

"Apart from Me you can do nothing." This is such a paradox, for obviously there is much we can do. But when we take action in our own strength, though the things we do may look like the fruit God wants to produce in our lives, they lack eternal value, and we will not experience His joy. Whether we build a dynamic church, spend hours in God's Word, or work our fingers to the bone in ministry, we labor in vain unless God has done it (Philippians 2:16; Psalm 127:1).

"Apart from Me you can do nothing." These words are like pruning shears to my heart as God reveals how much of my spiritual activity tends to be the result of fleshly fervor. Several months ago I wrestled with God over my purpose on this earth, feeling almost tormented by this fear. Before bed one night I told my husband that I felt depressed because God didn't need me and I no longer knew what to do. His answer disturbed me further still: "That's just it, you can't really do anything, can you?"

After tossing and turning all night, I cried out to God in prayer. Suddenly I saw my entire Christian life unfolding amid flames of fiery destruction. God spoke gently to my heart, revealing that He was burning up everything I had ever done in my own strength. I saw it all—my parenting, my marriage, my ministry, every study I'd ever taught, every word I'd written, every worship service I'd led, every time I'd witnessed, every conference I'd spoken at, every discipling relationship—all caught in a fire I couldn't contain. I could only weep. Finally in devastation, I cried out, "Lord, will there be anything left?"

Slowly the flames subsided, and out of the ashes one word arose: grace. Tenderly God assured me that by His grace there were things that had glorified Him. My heart trembled as He spoke: "What is left is what I have done through you; in fact, what I have done in spite of you." That graphic experience remains with me moment by moment, a haunting reminder that because I can do nothing without Christ, all that I do on my own will not last.

We Lay Down Our Worthiness

Similar to working hard for Jesus is our desire to be good enough for Him. We look at others who are more spiritual and feel undone by a load of guilt that destroys our passion. Or we see brothers and sisters who struggle in ways we don't and feel as if we can somehow take credit for having earned God's favor. This is so subtle it is almost impossible to recognize.

Often these attitudes have their roots in our earliest experiences as children. I learned at a young age that if I just did a little more, tried a little harder, and behaved a little better than my siblings, I could enjoy my parents' approval, which I confused with their love. Throughout my spiritual life as well, when my effort was greater than those of other believers, I felt a sense of spiritual superiority. I looked at their lack of discipline and admired my own diligence. I saw their emotional struggles and appreciated my stability. Underneath it all was the dangerous lie that God approved of me as long as I kept doing a little better than they did.

But the day finally came when I realized there were those whose spiritual walk far surpassed mine and no amount of effort would change that. My entire walk with God then came into question. For weeks I pleaded with Him to show me how to become more spiritual, how to attain a higher level of growth. The heavens were silent for days and days. When God finally spoke, my precious Father took me all the way back to my childhood, showing me how I'd come to relate to Him in ways that had nothing to do with grace. Over a period of weeks I learned for the first time the relief of inadequacy, the joy of being a helpless child.

During that time God showed me that in the story of the Prodigal Son, I was like the older brother. I read the father's words to the son who'd loyally served at home thinking this made him worthy of his inheritance, and I was completely taken aback. "Son, you have always been with me, and all that is mine is yours" (Luke 15:31).

The tragedy of coming to God on the basis of our own worth is not that He rejects us or disdains our diligence but that we simply cannot enjoy the inheritance He has already given us. "All that is mine is yours." God is the great provider—He has granted us *everything* pertaining to life and godliness (2 Peter 1:3), has given us *every* spiritual blessing in the heavenly places (Ephesians 1:3), and will supply *all* our needs (Philippians 4:19).

To be humble is to be a child, enjoying the wondrous inheritance that can never be called into question, for our heavenly Father has promised to perfect, confirm, strengthen, and establish us (1 Peter 5:10). Nothing frees us more to live in the wonder of grace like embracing the truth that "He who began a good work in [us] will perfect it until the day of Christ Jesus" (Philippians 1:6).

We Lay Down Our Talents and Abilities

Saul of Tarsus, to whom God appeared on the road to Damascus, was a devout Jew, fluent in both Greek and Hebrew, a Pharisee advanced beyond his peers in Judaism and extremely zealous for his ancestral traditions (Philippians 3:4–5; Galatians 1:13–14). Undoubtedly he was a man of great power and authority, well skilled in oratory and debate. What a contrast to the way the apostle Paul described himself to the church at Corinth:

> And when I came to you, brethren, I did not come with superiority of speech or of wisdom, proclaiming to you the testimony of God. For I determined to know nothing among you except Jesus Christ, and Him crucified. I was with you in *weakness and in fear and in much trembling*, and my message and my preaching were not in persuasive words of wisdom, but in demonstration of the Spirit and of power. (1 Corinthians 2:1–4)

Paul was a living testimony to the truth that God does not need our natural talents and abilities to accomplish His purposes. In fact, before they can be of any use to God, we must lay them at His feet, willing to leave them there unless He tells us to pick them up. It makes no difference how competent we are—whether speaking, singing, teaching, counseling, or even serving—if we are not simply empty vessels allowing God to use us, our talent will not glorify Him and is therefore a hindrance to His kingdom work.

In his first epistle, Peter wrote, "Whoever speaks, is to do so as one who is speaking the utterances of God; whoever serves is to do so as one who is serving by the strength which God supplies; so that in all things God may be glorified through Jesus Christ, to whom belongs the glory and dominion forever and ever. Amen" (4:11).

At the retreat I mentioned earlier, God sealed His lesson on humility in a heart-wrenching way. I struggle even now to write of this. The retreat chairman had told me they'd replaced my talk on Saturday night with a worship service so that a group of women who were leaving would not miss Communion. Deep in my heart, I was offended that they didn't care if the women missed what I had to say. God exposed this at the end of the retreat as women shared what the weekend had meant to them.

I waited for some to mention things I had taught, but most spoke instead of hearts changed by the Communion service. Painfully, God began to open my eyes to what I had done. I can still hear His voice: "You wanted it to be about you. You wanted it so badly that you even placed yourself above their remembrance of My death. Yet I can do more to change lives in one Eucharist than you can in all the talks you've ever done put together. It's not about you . . . it's all about Me."

That day a sense of fear and trembling invaded my heart. I now cry out daily in desperate dependence, for like Paul I am persuaded that my life and words have no power outside the anointing of God's Holy Spirit. As a parent, I can learn the skills to raise confident, productive children, but I cannot make them passionate about Jesus Christ. Date nights and marriage seminars in themselves can never guarantee God will be glorified through my marriage. In my writing or teaching or speaking, I can impart truth competently and possibly even build a reputation of excellence. But I cannot transform the people I minister to into the likeness of Christ. Whatever I do, however I might do it, if God is not working through me to glorify himself, then it will one day burn as rubble. Nothing has ever humbled me more than this truth.

What We Must Do

There seems to be a dearth of humility in the body of Christ today. Pious souls fight to maintain or regain our rights, pronouncing judgment on a perverse generation, but where are the humble ones whose gentleness compels others to take a second look? Strong servants work day and night with a tenacity that breeds self-confidence, but where are the needy ones who stand with heads bowed, empty-handed before almighty God? What will it take for us to embody the humble spirit of Christ?

We need to plead as John the Baptist did: "O God, You must increase but I must decrease" (John 3:30). When we do, we discover the precious peace of knowing that we have nothing to offer, while He has everything to give. We are incompetent, but He is adept; we are confused, but He is composed; we struggle and fail, but He has already won; we are inadequate, but He is able; we are feeble, but He is mighty. In all these things we overwhelmingly conquer, gladly boasting about our weaknesses, for through them He perfects His power within us (Romans 8:37; 2 Corinthians 12:9–10).

Come As a Child

There are several Greek and Hebrew words in Scripture that denote humility, but they all share the theme of lowliness. God brings down the high tree, and promises that every mountain and hill will be made low, and the first will be last in His kingdom (Ezekiel 17:24; Isaiah 40:4; Matthew 20:16). Jesus drove this point home by placing a small child in the midst of the disciples, telling them, "Whoever then humbles himself as this child, he is the greatest in the kingdom of heaven" (Matthew 18:4).

When Solomon took over the throne after his father, David, died, God appeared to him in a dream, asking him what he wanted above all else. Solomon offered praise to God for all He had done through his father, then humbly spoke: "I am but a little child; I do not know how to go out or come in" (1 Kings 3:7). The following verses tell us that God was pleased with Solomon's heart, promising to give him what he asked for and much, much more.

How different our Christian walk would be if we readily and continually admitted that we just don't know what we're doing. To be humble is to be lowly and needy by nature, dependent because we know no other way. There is tremendous joy and freedom in being childlike. We are no longer plagued with unrealistic expectations, nor do we strive to earn the Father's approval. We simply come as we are, trusting in and enjoying the love He has always shown us.

Brennan Manning, in his book *Abba's Child*, notes that while a Pharisee continually tries to induce God's love, a child assumes he already has it. He writes, "For the Pharisee, the emphasis is always on personal effort and achievement. The gospel of grace emphasizes the primacy of God's love. The Pharisee savors impeccable conduct; the child delights in the relentless tenderness of God."[3]

As children emptied of prideful independence, we find incredible hope, for the lower we are, the more God can fill us with himself. This is the amazing paradox of believing faith—that when we lower ourselves, "we go no longer down to nothing: our end is the beginning of a perfect union with God, the Beginner of Everything."[4]

Seek God's Face Rather Than Dwell on Our Sin

When I was in college, God did a great work on our campus, breaking many over their sin and calling them to himself. Soon a list of sins began to circulate to help others identify where they needed humbling. On several occasions I prayed through the list, but rather than being set free, I grew discouraged at the extent of my depravity. Today, in the growing movement of prayer for revival with its strong cry for broken hearts before God, I sense there are those who feel the way I did then. There is a subtle danger here. Andrew Murray noted, "Being occupied with self, even amid the deepest self-abhorrence, can never free us from self."[5]

So what do we do with sin? What is the humble response to our inevitable failure? Sin surely offends the heart of a holy God, so we never want to take it lightly. How are we to ensure that it is dealt with, yet not give in to an unhealthy obsession with our own shortcomings? We must remember that we are spiritual beings who, for now, battle this body of flesh. *We will sin.* If we deny it, we are deceived; if we ignore it, we risk grieving the Holy Spirit (1 John 1:8; Ephesians 4:22).

However, we are set free from sin not by dwelling on it but by gazing into the face of the One who has already paid the price. Seeing His grandeur, His perfection, His holy and pure love for ones like us cannot help but instill within us deep gratitude in light of our unworthiness. When this happens, we long to repent, to turn away from our sin, and live to please our precious Lord.

So instead of trying to stir up a sense of sinfulness, we call upon God's Spirit to do His work. While we invite conviction on the basis of His righteousness, we cry out at the same time for restoration on the basis of His mercy. If we don't do this, we will end up being endlessly self-absorbed, counteracting the very work God seeks to do in our hearts. All sin, though grievous to our souls, should only serve to catapult us to His side, ravenous for a touch of grace from "God, our only help against ourselves."[6]

Cling to the Crucified Lord

When my husband and I were in seminary, we started a weekly Bible study with a couple who lived nearby. He was a doctor who had rejected the Baptist teachings of his childhood, and she was a true agnostic, having no understanding of who Christ was. Each week the doctor and I enjoyed a hearty debate about issues such as abortion, capital punishment, and euthanasia, while our spouses watched quietly from the sidelines. One night God brought our table talk to a dramatic end.

Our normal debate mode had escalated into anger and then heavy silence when my husband quietly opened his Bible, reading the following words: "For I determined to know nothing among you except Jesus Christ, and Him crucified" (1 Corinthians 2:2). My heart grieved as I looked up and saw tears running down the cheeks of the doctor's wife. In all the weeks of study and discussion, she'd never responded to any truth we'd taught or debated. But in those few words the Cross was lifted up, shredding her defenses and breaking us both.

The Cross is a powerful weapon against pride. It is an awful thing that the living God suffered as He did; and when we see Him hanging there, our selfish agendas crumble at His nail-pierced feet. We simply cannot remain arrogant in the face of the One who humbled himself to the point of obedience on a cross. That encounter exposed the ugliness of my compulsion to interject opinions in every discussion. Whatever pleasure it had once given me was gone, leaving only a sick feeling in my soul.

How can we cling to our rights, when He gave up His? How can we demand the world's attention, when He received our scorn? How can we resent trying circumstances, when He left heaven's glory to dwell among us, wretched as we are? And how can we hang on to the misery of our old self, when He died that we might walk in newness of life?

To be humble, we must come to the Cross, over and over, day after day, contemplating our Savior whose humility resounds from the blows on His face, the stripes on His back, the holes in His hands and feet, and His side that was pierced through for our transgressions.

Trusting in Two Truths

In the corner of a churchyard outside of London stands a tombstone almost obscured by overgrown grass. It bears the following words:

John Newton, Clerk:
once an infidel and libertine,
a servant of slaves in Africa,
was by the rich mercy of our
Lord and Saviour Jesus Christ,
preserved, restored, pardoned,
and appointed to preach the faith
he had long labored to destroy.

This epitaph holds meaning for millions of believers since the early 1800s, for it tells of the man who wrote the hymn "Amazing Grace."

John Newton's life, before he came to Christ, was an odious one. His mother died when he was six, his father rejected him, and those with whom he had any relationship at all came to hate him for his vile behavior. But one day God used a violent storm at sea to bring him to faith, and from that point on he was never the same, working tirelessly for the needy and downtrodden.

As a minister, he wrote many hymns of deep gratitude for all God had done in his life. The words of his most famous one perhaps echo the cry of every heart that has ever grasped the wonder of redemption in Jesus Christ. Newton's tender awe can be felt in each line as he reminisces over his life:

Amazing grace! How sweet the sound,
that saved a wretch like me.
I once was lost but now am found,
was blind but now I see.
'Twas grace that taught my heart to fear,
and grace my fears relieved.
How precious did that grace appear,
the hour I first believed![7]

In his waning years, Newton told a friend, "My memory is nearly gone, but

I remember two things: that I am a great sinner, and that Christ is a great Savior."[8]

This is the heart of God's amazing grace. Precious, precious grace that draws us in like street urchins to a warm fire and a hearty meal, at a wedding feast beyond our wildest imaginings. In this we rest and rejoice, waiting for the moment we will see our Redeemer face-to-face. To be humble is to live always with poignant awareness of God's extravagant grace poured out in exchange for our complete inadequacy.

TAKING UP OUR CROSS—
What We Gain and What We Lose

To a world that glorifies self, humility is an enigma. It is a complete paradox that the first shall be last, the meek shall inherit the earth, and the abased shall be exalted. But this is the birthright of the humble soul, and the treasures humility obtains are beyond imagination.

Gain Honor

"Before destruction the heart of man is haughty, but humility goes before honor" (Proverbs 18:12).

"The reward of humility and the fear of the Lord are riches, honor and life" (Proverbs 22:4).

Lose Humiliation

"But when you are invited, go and recline at the last place, so that when the one who has invited you comes, he may say to you, 'Friend, move up higher'; then you will have honor in the sight of all who are at the table with you. For everyone who exalts himself will be humbled, and he who humbles himself will be exalted" (Luke 14:10–11).

Living for the affirmation of others will make us miserable. God offers a far better plan. To be humble is to die to the desire for human praise, which is often hollow and fickle, and to open ourselves to the joy of God's favor—the unconditional eternal applause of heaven.

Gain God's Favor

"How blessed are the people who know the joyful sound! O Lord, they walk in the light of your countenance. In your name they rejoice all the day, and by your righteousness they are exalted. For you are the glory of their strength, and by your favor our horn is exalted" (Psalm 89:15–17).

Lose False Security

"How can you believe, when you receive glory from one another and you do not seek the glory that is from the one and only God?" (John 5:44).

"For am I now seeking the favor of men, or of God? Or am I striving to please men? If I were still trying to please men, I would not be a bond-servant of Christ" (Galatians 1:10).

The old adage "Laugh and the world laughs with you, cry and you cry alone" is a painful testimony of the capricious nature of worldly success. No matter how high we rise, when we fall, judgment and disrespect are our lot. The fear of failure is an albatross from which we can be freed as we let go of pride, learning to rest in the abundant adequacy that God provides.

Gain Confidence

"Such confidence we have through Christ toward God. Not that we are adequate in ourselves to consider anything as coming from ourselves, but our adequacy is from God" (2 Corinthians 3:4–5).

Lose Fear of Failure

"Pride goes before destruction, and a haughty spirit before stumbling" (Proverbs 16:18).

"The Lord is the one who goes ahead of you; He will be with you. He will not fail you or forsake you. Do not fear or be dismayed" (Deuteronomy 31:8).

The self-made man is pompous and unpleasant. Believing he is the source of all things, he takes advantage of others, acting as if the fate of the world is in his hands. But to the one who knows that each breath is a gift from God, all things are a blessing; everything that happens offers a reason for thanksgiving.

Gain Gratitude
"From them will proceed thanksgiving and the voice of those who celebrate; and I will multiply them and they will not be diminished; I will also honor them and they will not be insignificant" (Jeremiah 30:19).

Lose Presumption
"And when your herds and your flocks multiply, and your silver and gold multiply, and all that you have multiplies, then your heart will become proud and will forget the Lord your God" (Deuteronomy 8:13–14).

To live with pride is to box life into predictable patterns that enable us to keep up a good front. We must keep our backs covered, for the danger that the truth will be known and our masks ripped off lurks in every task and relationship. Grace is so different. It uncovers all, bathing our lives in waves of blessing, filling our hearts with the wonder of what we've received.

Gain Wonder
"When I consider Your heavens, the work of Your fingers, the moon and the stars, which You have ordained, what is man that You take thought of him, and the son of man that you care for him?" (Psalm 8:3–4).

Lose Pride

"But He gives a greater grace. Therefore it says, 'God is opposed to the proud, but gives grace to the humble'" (James 4:6).

Can you imagine holding on to pride, suffering humiliation, living in fear of failure, and clinging to false security, all the while projecting a haughty, presumptuous spirit? There is no more miserable way to live. As believers, we take up our cross against all of this, letting God pour into our lives honor, confidence, and favor, which daily replenish us with gratitude and wonder.

PRACTICING HUMILITY— A Mini-Retreat

Because all sin, one way or another, is rooted in pride, we must deal with it if we are to live victoriously in Christ. Scripture tells us over and over that we are blind, deaf, and hardhearted when it comes to seeing our own pride. We are completely dependent on His Spirit to reveal the truth about this and illuminate our hearts to receive it.

Preparing Your Heart

To begin, wait in silence before God for at least five minutes. Set your mind on Him, only offering short words of adoration or praise as you feel led. Breathe deeply and evenly, settling your physical body before Him. When you have *stilled and quieted your soul*, ask the Holy Spirit to open the eyes of your heart today to all He wants to show you. Thank Him in advance that He will do this.

Read Psalm 130 aloud slowly. As you read it the second time, consider the following questions:

Why does David cry out?

How does he wait?

What gives him hope?

Meditate on the psalm and write a prayer of gratitude in your prayer journal.

Contemplating His Presence

Read Luke 18:9–14 and Matthew 9:10–13 in preparation for this time of meditation.

So often we view the Pharisees of Scripture with disdain, appalled at their arrogant behavior. But if we look closely, we might see in them a little of ourselves. Perhaps their rigid adherence to the law was simply their way of living out a faith that had lost its passion. Without the joy of intimacy with God, what other motivation could they rely on than a standard of excellence they thought made them worthy to be called His own?

We too slip into forms of behavior that have little to do with grace. Instead of the easy yoke to which Christ calls us, we wear a difficult one that has been formed through years of our own religious traditions, not realizing that this isn't the way it's supposed to be. But when our service to God has become dry and barren, when we find ourselves laboring with little joy for His kingdom, when we are motivated by anything other than a heart filled with wonder, then perhaps we have become the Pharisees for whom Jesus reserved His strongest admonitions. Consider these things as you read and contemplate the following scenario.

> The church is full tonight and there is a spirit of expectancy in the air. You got here a little late, hoping you could just slip quietly into the pew instead of engaging in small talk. It's not that you don't care about people, but most of the time you get a lot more out of hearing a good message from the Word. Sometimes you wish you could stay home from prayer meeting, but you know you shouldn't feel that way, so you always show up.
>
> As the prayers begin, you join in, nodding and saying amen at the ap-

propriate times. But when one person goes into a long discourse, your mind wanders. You feel such relief that your life is so stable, so well ordered. How glad you are that you don't have to confess sin week after week like some who just can't seem to get their lives on track.

Your reverie is suddenly interrupted as you hear the pastor call your name, asking you to end the time of prayer with a season of thanksgiving. Sighing, you stand, glad the meeting is almost over.

"Father," you begin with an appropriately reverent voice.

"Thank you for your goodness to me. I thank you that you saved me when I was young and my life has always seen your blessing . . . I praise you for the time I've spent with you this week. Thank you for giving me a heart to pray and for all the blessings I have received from my fast this month."

You continue on, the cadence of your voice having found a comfortable rhythm.

"I praise you for the soul that might be added to your kingdom from this afternoon when you nudged me to witness to the grocery store clerk . . . Lord, there are many in our body who don't know the reward of being at this prayer meeting, but I know you're pleased with those who've made the sacrifice to come."

Heartfelt amens resound around you as your words carry an appealing energy. But as you start to speak again, you find your mouth will not open. An odd quiet descends on the room, your heart beating wildly. Then you hear these words: "I didn't come for the healthy."

The voice is unlike anything you've ever heard—so gentle, yet compelling. Fearful, you want to run, but you can't move at all. You feel completely alone. Again, the voice speaks, now calling your name: "I didn't come for the healthy."

This time the words touch a deep place in your soul, a place hardened from years of service and fear of being exposed. Tears well up in you, finally spilling out in waves of emotion. Unable to do anything else, you fall down, your neediness clutching your heart until you can stand it no longer.

"Oh, God, be merciful to me, for I am a sinner. . . ."

The words echo from within you like the wail of a woman in labor. Face pressed to the ground, you feel as if you can never look up again. You hear it again, but this time the voice of God descends like a blanket of peace surrounding your soul and comforting your heart.

"I didn't come for the healthy, I came for sinners like you. Now you are righteous before me . . . now I can lift you to the heights of glorious grace I've longed to see you live in. Never forget that I came for the needy, the helpless, the desperate, the lonely, the broken, the tormented, and the anxious. If you will let me, I will pour the oil of grace into the wounds of pride you've worn for so long. I did not come for the healthy . . . I came for this . . ."

Responding to His Call

Spend a period of time asking God to reveal the neediness of your own heart. Receive His ministry to you.

Spend the final time in thanksgiving and adoration for our unfathomable God who deserves all the glory and willingly gives himself freely to us. Use the following Scriptures as a basis: 1 Chronicles 29:11–16; Ephesians 3:20–21; Jude 24–25.

Going Forward

What wonder we experience in trading our deficiency, our weakness, our inadequacy, and our faults for the fullness of an eternal God. Though we long to please Him, we are never surprised when we don't. Though we seek to make Him Lord, we rest in grace at each new level of growth, aware of but not distressed by how far we have to go. These things are the seeds of inner peace, the hope for a quiet heart in the midst of a very disquieted world. Let us discover the blessing of quietness.

Notes

1. As quoted by Jill Haak Adels in *Wisdom of the Saints* (New York: Oxford University Press, 1987), 129.
2. Words taken from "Jesus, Lover of My Soul" by Paul Oakley. Used by permission.
3. Manning, 89.
4. Walt Wangerin, *Reliving the Passion* (Grand Rapids: Zondervan, 1992).
5. Andrew Murray, *Humility* (London: Oliphante, Limited, n.d.), 65.
6. Fenelon, 99.
7. John Newton, "Amazing Grace" (public domain).
8. Billy Graham, *Crusade Hymn Stories* (Carol Stream, Ill.: Hope Publishing Company, 1967), 8.

CHAPTER FIVE

QUIETNESS

*In that moment of quietness, there is a transaction from the way of
self to the way of God. It is not a time when we seek to change God's
attitude toward us; rather we are changing our attitude toward Him.*[1]

Harold Rogers

It was springtime in the Canadian Rockies, and God's astonishing handiwork
enveloped me with a sense of wonder. The morning sun danced across the
horizon, drenching everything from the snow-capped mountains to the ver-
dant meadows below. I stood in quiet awe, my soul confirming the seraphim's
cry that indeed "the whole earth is full of God's glory" (Isaiah 6:3).

A creek rushed several feet below me, its current pulsing with intensity.
I walked along the trail above, eager to see where it might take me. As I
rounded the next bend, the trail and the creek came to an abrupt end at a
breathtaking sight. From a towering cliff, a massive waterfall pounded, its
mist-saturated roar filling the air.

To my right was a small cave-like opening, and as I stepped through it,
I found myself only a few feet from the base of the falls. Nothing could have
prepared me for that encounter, where tons of water thundered within my
reach, tumultuous and testy, striking a strange fear within me. I wanted to
escape, to back right out through the tiny opening, but I felt powerless. My
heart pounding in my chest, it seemed as if the waterfall had cast a spell on
me. Transfixed, I stood in silence and finally, after being soaked to the bone,
managed to withdraw.

"Deep calls to deep at the sound of Thy waterfalls" (Psalm 42:7). That day, and for many to follow, the words of the psalmist echoed in my ears along with the memory of my gloriously odd epiphany. Since then God has begun to show me that what I felt in those moments was not unlike my relationship with Him. He is powerful in ways that can terrify me, making me want to run and hide, yet at the same time He draws me in, comforting me somehow with His splendid strength.

Because of this, my walk with God has been an extraordinary adventure, seeming at times to be fraught with danger and at others punctuated with delight. Things don't usually go according to plan, at least not the one I think is in place. I agree with Harold Myra, who wrote, "This call to adventure has been a strange mixture of tedium, trauma, accomplishment, anger, frustration, amazement, ecstasy, and bewilderment. . . . God is not, as C. S. Lewis indicates, a tame lion."[2]

I share this experience with the same sort of trepidation I feel in writing about quietness, for I had expected this subject to be simple and straightforward—filled with gentle admonitions to get away from the noise of a clamorous culture and discover the rest of a more contemplative pace. But as enticing as that message might have been, in the end it would have lacked a basis in reality for those who get up each morning to face a world that feels far more like a rat race than a walk in the park.

The Bible speaks of quietness fairly often but almost never in the context of withdrawal. The *rest* Scripture promises takes place more often in the midst of a storm than through the absence of troubled waters. Thus my waterfall in the Rockies sheds some light on this treacherous tightrope we must walk if we would follow Christ. For somehow quietness comes by learning to live in the tension of trusting a God so powerful He can do anything He wants, yet so unpredictable He almost never does what we think He should. "To fear and not be afraid—that is the paradox of faith."[3] And that is the dilemma that confronts us as we pursue this elusive virtue.

Foundations for Quietness

Sovereign.
My God is sovereign.
My God can do what He wants to do,
when He wants to do it.
So why should I be offended?

Alternating between swelling emotion and whispers of wonder, the five-part Gospel group at our local community college Christmas concert passionately poured out their souls with these words, and I was deeply moved. Glancing around, I noticed others equally taken. Tears streamed down some cheeks, a few rocked back and forth nodding, while many tendered hearty amens.

In a crescendo of intricate harmony, the song ended, and we all rose to our feet with exclamations more like worship than applause. The message had found a home in this audience. *Sovereign. My God is sovereign. . . .* This thought touches some deep place, as if to comfort the child within each of us who longs for a Father big enough to beat the schoolyard bullies. But what does God's sovereignty really mean?

Though Scripture is replete with references to God's sovereignty, in only one instance is the word "sovereign" actually given as a name for God. According to the *New American Standard Bible* translation, Paul describes Christ as the blessed and only Sovereign. In this verse, he uses the Greek word *dunastes* (the same as the Latin root for our word "dynamite"), referring to a ruler with ultimate power. Yet even Paul could not just say "Sovereign" and leave it at that. He added, as if by explanation, "King of kings and Lord of lords, who alone possesses immortality and dwells in unapproachable light, whom no man has seen or can see. To Him be honor and eternal dominion! Amen" (1 Timothy 6:15–16).

The sovereignty of God is critical to the issue of quietness, and thus we must spend some time there. Though it is so vast and complex that we will never fully grasp its import until we see Him in the fullness of His glory, there are a few components that might be helpful to see.

God Is Eternal, Omniscient, and Omnipotent

God's sovereignty means that He is infinite and eternal. He is *I AM*, the Alpha and the Omega, who is and who was and who is to come (Revelation 1:8). At some point in the distant expanse of the past, God made the world and all things in it. He alone gives every being life and breath and determines the appointed times for every person (Acts 17:24–26). His Word says He is so exalted we can never fully know Him or comprehend the length of His existence (Job 36:26).

God's sovereignty also means He knows all things. As a God of knowledge, He weighs all our actions (1 Samuel 2:3). He knows every move before we make it and every word before we speak it (Psalm 139:3–4). His eyes are in every place at every moment (Proverbs 15:3). Can you begin to imagine such a thing? God possesses all knowledge at every moment in time—His knowledge is immeasurable.

Finally, God's sovereignty means He holds all power. His Word tells us, in fact, that power belongs only to Him (Psalm 62:11). His power knows no limits (Numbers 11:23), and when He stretches out His hand, no one can turn it back or frustrate His plans (Isaiah 14:27). Nothing is impossible to Him (Matthew 19:26).

God goes to great lengths to assure us of His sovereign nature—He is eternal, omniscient, and omnipotent. He cannot be contained nor limited by our understanding or our desires. He is the *I AM*. Charles Spurgeon once said of God's sovereignty: "It is not a light or trifling matter, it is a truth that, above all others, should stir the depths of our nature."

God Will Accomplish His Purposes

Several years ago Rabbi Harold Kushner penned the book *When Bad Things Happen to Good People*. Addressing the issue of pain and suffering,

Rabbi Kushner proposed the idea that though God created the world, He now watches from a distance, hands necessarily removed. He concludes that though God hates evil as much as we do, He is powerless over it, for it is simply the logical course and destiny of man created with free will.

Today the book remains a bestseller, encouraging people with its simple explanation. Comforting though it might seem, Kushner's idea of a hands-off God does not square with Scripture. God makes it clear that He is purposeful and actively involved in all things. He "works all things after the counsel of His will" and "whatever the Lord pleases He does" (Ephesians 1:11; Psalm 135:6). God avows that He alone puts to death, gives life, wounds and heals, and no one can deliver from His hand (Deuteronomy 32:39). He makes poor and rich and brings low and exalts (1 Samuel 2:6–8).

Some contend that God causes all things, while others feel He only allows, but for all practical purposes, it makes little difference. He is omnipotent and thus able to do whatever He wants to do. God himself pointed out Job to Satan, permitting him to bring him harm. Yet God made it clear that the boundaries were in His hand, not the Evil One's: "Behold, all that he [Job] has is in your power, only do not put forth your hand on him" (Job 1:12).

Toward the end of Job's terrifying trials, God finally settles every question Job has had through a lengthy oration of His infinite attributes and ways. As God finishes, an awestruck Job answers: "I know that You can do all things, and that no purpose of yours can be thwarted" (Job 42:2).

God will accomplish His purposes—His Word affirms this over and over. He speaks through the prophet Isaiah that there is no other God, nor one like Him, who can declare the end from the beginning and things that haven't happened yet from ancient times. Because of this, He reminds us, "My purpose will be established, and I will accomplish all my good pleasure. . . . Truly I have spoken, truly I will bring it to pass. I have planned it, surely I will do it" (Isaiah 46:10–11).

Because God Is Good, His Purposes Are Good

Whether the truth of God's sovereign power will comfort or fill our hearts with fear depends largely on whether we believe He is good. If He is not good, then He is capricious and with no moral basis does whatever He fancies at the moment. This would be a frightening god to serve and the world he runs a terrifying place to live.

But Scripture clearly asserts that God is good, an attribute that was often in full view when Yahweh revealed himself to the Israelites. When Moses asked to see God's glory, He responded, "I Myself will make all My goodness pass before you" (Exodus 33:19). At the dedication of the temple, Solomon prayed a lengthy prayer ending with: "O Lord God, be clothed with salvation and let your godly ones rejoice in what is good." Then the glory of God appeared and the people fell on their faces in worship, crying out, "Truly He is good, truly His lovingkindness is everlasting!" (2 Chronicles 6:41; 7:3).

If God is inherently good, then His purposes must be good, His power being used to accomplish them. Often Scripture speaks of God's sovereign power directly in connection with the good things He has done or will do for His people. Psalm 103, a litany of praise, speaks in the first eighteen verses of the goodness of God, beginning with an admonition to bless the Lord and not forget His benefits. Consider this incredible list:

- Who pardons all your iniquities, who heals all your diseases.
- Who redeems your life from the pit, who crowns you with lovingkindness and compassion.
- Who satisfies your years with good things, so that your youth is renewed like the eagle.
- The Lord performs righteous deeds and judgments for all who are oppressed.
- He made known His ways to Moses, His acts to the sons of Israel.
- The Lord is compassionate and gracious, slow to anger and abounding in lovingkindness.

- He will not always strive with us nor will He keep His anger forever.

- He has not dealt with us according to our sins nor rewarded us according to our iniquities.

- For as high as the heavens are above the earth, so great is His loving-kindness toward those who fear Him.

- As far as the east is from the west, so far has He removed our transgressions from us.

- Just as a father has compassion on his children, so the Lord has compassion on those who fear Him.

- For He himself knows our frame; He is mindful that we are but dust (vv. 1–16).

Then, to make sure we understand that God is not only good but also has the power to do all these things for us, David adds: "The Lord has established His throne in the heavens, and His sovereignty rules over all" (v. 19).

Though we may never fully understand the mystery of a good God who allows bad things to happen, and while theologians may endlessly debate the inferences of God permitting evil on this earth, in the end we must simply trust in His Word. "No one is good but God Himself," Jesus asserted.

Thus God will accomplish His purposes, always acting out of His infinite goodness, guided by His limitless knowledge, and empowered by His absolute might. "More than that no one knows at present; and more than that no one needs to know. The name of God is sufficient guarantee of the perfection of His works."[4]

QUIETNESS

*A pervasive inner calm that comes as we
learn to rest in the arms of our sovereign Lord.*

Barriers to Quietness

So often we speak of God in grandfatherly terms that fail to reflect the battle that rages in our hearts. We affirm that He is a shelter from the storm, but what if He is the very storm from which we feel we need relief? We hide beneath His wings, but what do we do when He, flapping wild pinions, soars out across a vast and black expanse? Can we as easily claim that He is good and faithful and wise and powerful during the winter of our soul's discontent as we do during the dog days of summer?

To learn the art of quietness might require something akin to molting—a shedding of our warm, comfortable skin to expose a more appropriate one for the climate in which we find ourselves. To find the *rest* our birthright as believers guarantees, we're going to have to walk right up to the God who has issued the invitation and face head on the fears we face in light of His sovereignty, power, and goodness. Three fears that will surely thwart any hope of experiencing quietness are the fear of losing faith, the fear of losing control, and the fear of pain.

Fear of Losing Faith

Recently in a discussion my husband had with a leader of a widespread prayer movement, he mentioned that he believed the greatest problem facing the church today is a loss of hope. It was an intriguing thought. He shared how people had prayed for so long, and when the inactive God of their experience didn't seem to match the all-powerful God of Scripture, they simply gave up hope, their faith subtly slipping into a malaise characterized by dry works and heartless duty.

The authors of *The Sacred Romance* speak of a similar thing, suggesting that many professing Christians have become *practical agnostics*, who live as if it doesn't matter whether God shows up or not, protecting their faith just in case He doesn't. Here's how they describe the thinking that represents our struggle:

He can spin the earth, change the weather, topple governments, obliterate armies, and resurrect the dead. Is it too much to ask that He intervene in our story? But he often seems aloof, almost indifferent to our plight, so entirely out of our control. Would it be any worse if there were no God? If He didn't exist, at least we wouldn't get our hopes up. We could settle once and for all that we really are alone in the universe and get on with surviving as best we may.[5]

When God does not seem to come through in our lives or when something about His character revealed through Scripture doesn't square with our experience, we are tempted to redefine Him in less troublesome ways. This is why many Christians who were more comfortable with an impotent God than one who could stop the evil in the world, but doesn't, embraced Rabbi Kushner's book.

This fear, though it may guard our hearts against disappointment with God, carries with it an undercurrent of anxiety. Once we doubt God's sovereignty, we inevitably question His other attributes, such as His love or faithfulness or wisdom. *God—why?* becomes the painful lament of our lives as we lose all sense of divine perspective.

Isaiah 40 is an amazing litany of God's power, knowledge, and eternal character, as I noted in the first chapter. At the end of His weighty interchange with Isaiah, God addresses the Israelites' personal battle over faith. They were disturbed at God's seeming lack of concern and fretting over their need because they failed to understand the magnitude of His greatness. He questions them poignantly, "O Jacob, O Israel, how can you say that the Lord doesn't see your troubles and isn't being fair? Don't you yet understand? Don't you know by now that the everlasting God, the Creator of the farthest parts of the earth, never grows faint or weary? No one can fathom the depths of his understanding" (Isaiah 40:27–28, TLB).

When we ascribe more manageable, more easily acceptable attributes to God in order to protect our faith, we miss out on the comfort He longs to give. This fear will rob our hearts of quietness and deadlock our walk with God in tragic ways.

Fear of Losing Control

Mother Teresa wrote that some of the most powerful advice anyone ever gave her was to "let Jesus use you without consulting you."[6] When I first read this, I had to laugh, but on deeper thought realized it reflects one of my lifelong struggles—a desire to be in control. Fear of losing control is a destructive force that keeps us from experiencing the peace of resting in God's plans and purposes.

High-control people are some of the most anxiety-ridden on the planet. Some of us just like to be in charge, thinking we do a better job than others. Our fear of losing control is based on arrogance fed by selfish agendas. As one pastor said, "We all like to be little sovereigns." For many others, though, the fear has its basis in some past and perhaps painful experience. Somewhere along the line we may have learned that not being in control might result in a loss of safety or security or protection from harm. We believe, therefore, that being the master of our own fate, though extremely stressful, is less agonizing than the real or perceived alternatives.

King Solomon said, "One hand full of rest is better than two fists full of labor and striving after wind" (Ecclesiastes 4:6). When we cling to control, we are driven by our fear, two-fisted in our striving against anything that interferes with our agenda. This fear, perhaps more consistently than any other, keeps us from resting in our Father's arms. If we don't believe He will protect us, then we cannot let Him have His way in our lives. We end up rejecting God's sovereignty "because we know if God gets His will, we may not get our own."[7]

One morning in prayer as I read Psalm 97, God addressed my rugged determination to have my own way: "The Lord reigns, let the earth rejoice, let the many islands be glad." The next verse stopped me in my tracks: "Clouds and thick darkness surround Him." I became very still, sensing

God's presence as I read the next passages quietly in meditation. "Fire goes before Him and burns up His adversaries round about. His lightnings lit up the world; the earth saw and trembled. The mountains melted like wax at the presence of the Lord." As God began to open my heart, revealing the profundity of those words, I literally started to tremble myself. Later I wrote in my prayer journal:

> *Lord, I in my sinful state cannot fully view your reign—I would be consumed, destroyed by your glory. You are sovereign and I dare not bristle at this—for I am not invited to share your reign. You rule in my heart and though I cannot always pierce the clouds that surround your glory, I must rest in knowing that you are sovereign.*
>
> *I am vain to think I can understand you.*
> *I am wretched to fret and fume.*
> *I am foolish to tell you what to do.*
>
> *Human arrogance denigrates your reign, for I cannot see through the clouds and darkness that stand between my sin and your glory. Oh, my God, how dare I try?*

When we resist God's sovereignty, suppressing our fears and denying our pride, our hearts will be like "the tossing sea, for it cannot be quiet, and its waters toss up refuse and mud" (Isaiah 57:20). But the omnipotent and always good God longs to be the strong tower to whom we continually run. Moment by moment He cries out to our fearful souls, *O people, pour out your heart before Me; I am a refuge for you* (Psalm 62:8).

Fear of Pain

Closely related to our fear of losing control is our fear of pain. Though no one would say they enjoy suffering, because the Western world places an inordinate value on health and physical strength, our fears can become greatly magnified. If we view suffering as a terrible thing or the result of God punishing us for some wrong we've done, we will avoid it at all costs.

This only intensifies our agitation at this inevitable condition of life. M. Scott Peck wrote in *The Road Less Traveled*, "Life is difficult . . . once we truly know that life is difficult—once we truly understand and accept it— then life is no longer difficult."[8]

The fear of pain causes a continual war with God over the circumstances of our lives, robbing us of peace. Over and over, God gently chides His people not to fear the things this world can do to us. And over and over He tells us we belong to Him and therefore He will always be with us. In one tender exhortation, He cried out to the Israelites:

> But now, thus says the Lord, your Creator, O Jacob, and He who formed you, O Israel, "Do not fear, for I have redeemed you; I have called you by name; you are Mine! When you pass through the waters, I will be with you; and through the rivers, they will not overflow you. When you walk through the fire, you will not be scorched, nor will the flame burn you" (Isaiah 43:1–2).

Not long ago several pieces of my life were in great disarray. It seemed as if God had walked away after tossing my dreams up in the air, letting them fall in all directions. I prayed for understanding but, finding none, became agitated and distraught. I wanted action or answers and was getting neither. One night I awoke with these words pounding in my mind: *Even the wind and the seas obey Him*.

I got up, sensing that God would show me something through the story of the disciples tossing on the stormy sea while Jesus slept. As I read, I saw myself clearly. When the boat was about to go under, and they had reached their wits' end, the disciples woke Jesus up, then were amazed when He calmed the storm. "Who then is this, that He commands even the winds and the water, and they obey Him?" (Luke 8:24–25).

Fear of pain is a great barrier to living in the comfort of God's sovereignty. Jesus told the disciples they should never fear those who might destroy the body but instead fear God who has ultimate power to destroy both their body and soul in hell (Matthew 10:28). Illustrating His omniscience, He told how His Father never missed the death of a sparrow and He knew the number of hairs on every one of their heads. Tenderly He assured them, "So do not fear, you are more valuable than many sparrows." Amid the fierce storms of life, atop the crashing course of wave after wave of pain, we can rest in our worth to a sovereign God—*for even the wind and the seas obey Him*.

What We Must Do

It almost seems an oxymoron to speak of *doing* in relationship to quietness. In truth, there is far less for us to do than to *be*. Quietness will never come from simply knowing truth or even committing to it in faith. Quietness is the result of relationship with God, of living in the warmth of His embrace, learning to receive His love and loving Him in return. Madame Guyon, a godly sixteenth-century Frenchwoman who suffered immensely throughout her life, wrote in a letter to a friend:

How I wish you would comprehend how good God is and how perfectly He guards what belongs to Him! How jealous and how watchful He is over us! Let God become everything to you. See nothing, love nothing, want nothing but what He wants you to see, love or want. Let Him become so much to you that it becomes easy to love and submit to Him. Trust God as if you were blindfolded. Trust Him without questioning or reasoning. God is! This is enough.[9]

Indeed, it is enough. But how do we come to this place of abandonment? What do we need to see or grab on to? Three things can encourage us: Learn to anticipate God's amazing surprises, trust in His unfolding plan, and rest in His sovereign goodness. These are the seeds that, implanted within, can blossom into the fruit of a quiet heart.

Anticipate God's Amazing Surprises

I went today to a convalescent hospital, the recent home of my ninety-five-year-old grandmother. It has been so hard to watch this once strong and passionate woman's health fail, her body shrinking to skin and bones and her mind drifting in and out of reality. Twice she has fallen, each time her days descending further into a rhythm of drug-induced stupor and excruciating pain.

At first I found myself arguing with God all the way home each time I visited. It seemed so senseless—these lives that once held hope and purpose now caught in a web of what appeared to be endless futility. But then something happened to Mabel, my grandmother's roommate, that silenced my protests.

At lunch one day, Mabel commented to a friend of mine who'd come along, "I've never met anyone quite like Frances. She is so kind and always so happy."

My friend responded, "You know why, don't you?" Then, turning to my grandmother, she asked, "It's because of Jesus, isn't it, Frances?"

For the next several minutes, with glowing face, Grandmother talked of her relationship with God. When she finished, my friend asked Mabel if she would like to give her life to Christ as well. Mabel was one of God's amazing surprises, for at ninety years old she was born again. One of the most assuring consequences of God's sovereignty is that He is always at work, accomplishing His purposes.

From the daily irritations of a dryer on the blink, crashing computers, and changes in our children's soccer schedule, to the grueling realities of financial ruin or loved ones facing death, the circumstances of our lives assault us at times like a dissonant chorus. Yet walking with Christ can turn each situation into a surprising adventure, for if we watch we just may see His hand in ways we would never have dreamed.

This enables us to live with a sense of *joyful uncertainty*, sort of like "standing on tiptoe to see what God is going to do next, even in the worst of circumstances."[10] Joyful uncertainty is a good description for the way we feel when God begins to work His quietness into our hearts. We may not have a clue as to why God is doing what He is doing, but the unknown no longer has the power to agitate us.

Instead, we delight in discovering the "treasures of darkness and the hidden wealth of secret places," for it is our precious Lord who walks with us, calling us by name, teaching us from His own heart (Isaiah 45:3). No longer are "we concerned with the instrument God uses to speak to us, whether the pencil writes in blue ink or green, but with what God is saying to us."[11]

And speak He will, surprising us when we least expect it. For, indeed, "the Lord longs to be gracious to you, and therefore He waits on high to have compassion on you. For the Lord is a God of justice; how blessed are all those who long for Him" (Isaiah 30:18). What an assurance this brings, and how it can quiet our hearts in the midst of the chaos and clutter of life in this world.

Trust in God's Unfolding Plan

In 1956 five young American men left everything to take the gospel to the Huaorani Indians in Ecuador. Before they ever preached their first sermon, all five were brutally murdered by the tribe.[12] At the time the murders seemed senseless and without any redeeming purpose. To human understanding, all that was known was that five men had died in God's service, leaving four widows and nine fatherless children.

However, as the years unfolded, it became clear that God was using the situation to spread Christianity to that entire area of the world and raise up hundreds of American young people who would likewise leave everything for the sake of Christ. In 1996 Steve Saint (son of the murdered Nate Saint) revealed previously unknown details of the story, which show even more the magnificence of God's plan.

Steve and his family went to live among the now predominantly Christian tribe some years ago at the tribe's request. One afternoon in a dialogue with some of the tribal leaders, the story of what really happened on that ominous day forty years ago began to come out. Though they'd never discussed it before, the five men and women seemed compelled to talk about it with Steve.

He writes that in hearing their story, it became clear to him that there was really no logical reason the murders had taken place outside of divine intervention. In other words, the son of one of the missionaries who was killed that day says God purposed it to happen. As proof, he shares an astounding new piece of the story. One of the women told him that after all were dead, she heard a noise and looked up to see Cowodi (foreigners) singing above the trees. Two of the other men affirmed that they too had heard the music and saw lights like a sky full of jungle beetles. Later, when Elizabeth Elliot came to live among them, they remembered this and, believing the truths she shared, gave their lives to Christ.

As players in a drama that at times looks like a tragedy, we take great comfort in knowing how the play ends. The rest of the world may look at our lives and see reason to despair, but we know that reality doesn't rest in what the eye can see. We can daily rejoice that our God reigns, that our time on this earth is merely a blip on eternity's screen. Our rest comes in knowing that all things do indeed work for good in our lives, for daily we are being made more like Jesus. And one day, when we see Him face-to-face, the puzzle we have called life will be put together, every piece making perfect sense, every struggle we've known fitting beautifully into a timeless tapestry of God's sovereign grace. Steve Saint concludes:

> God took five common young men of uncommon commitment and used them for His own glory. They never had the privilege they so enthusiastically pursued to tell the Huaorani of the God they loved and served. But for every Huaorani who today follows God's trail through the efforts of others, there are a thousand Cowodi who follow God's trail more resolutely because of their example. This suc-

cess, withheld from them in life, God multiplied and continues to multiply as a memorial to their obedience and faithfulness.[13]

Rest in God's Sovereign Goodness

In the midst of dark uncertainty, when the strain of living in a fallen world threatens to overwhelm us, God challenges us to gaze out over the horizon like children who wait at the window for their father to come home. With expectancy we watch and wait, not knowing when He will come, but finding comfort in the assurance that He always does.

Perhaps the most difficult thing about resting is the time we must spend with no answers, the ongoing, aching reality that the "silence of a wise and good God is shattering."[14] But if we long to see God accomplish His purposes in our lives, the seasons of waiting will be many. Often God reveals His plan only to bring circumstances our way that make it seem impossible. "Wait" may be God's favorite word. Perhaps it is because He is not limited by time, or maybe He is more concerned with the process in our hearts than the outcome. But whatever the reason, God just doesn't seem to be in a hurry.

God showed Abraham a vast land that would become the dwelling of His people, but it was four hundred years before the Hebrew children actually entered Canaan. He called the young shepherd boy David from the fields to be King of Israel, then made him spend years as a fugitive and outlaw, waiting until he was thirty years old to begin his reign. He gave Joseph his dreams as a young boy, then allowed him to be beaten, imprisoned, falsely accused, and given servant's status for years before fulfilling the dreams. Prophet after prophet in the Old Testament spoke God's words of impending judgment, then became laughingstocks or targets of abuse when it wasn't forthcoming.

How do we rest in God's goodness when He seems to be doing nothing? How do we avoid becoming "alternately rebellious runaways and whining babies"?[15] We can learn from God's words to the Israelites, who faced certain destruction as the mighty war machine of Assyria advanced upon them. Terrified, they turned to the strong but pagan nation of Egypt, joining forces against their common foe. God was furious. After admonishing them for their foolish plan, He spoke: "In repentance and rest you will be saved, in quietness and trust is your strength. But you were not willing" (Isaiah 30:15).

Repentance and rest . . . quietness and trust. For those who struggle, this is a tall order, an impossible one, creating perhaps another kind of tension. Bob Sorge, a pastor who has suffered from a grievous physical condition for several years, tells of trying to find the balance of being both quiet and confident: "It's very much like a paradox. In calling us to quietness and confidence simultaneously, God is basically saying, 'Get your focus back on Me, see Me with all your heart, renew your confidence that I will deliver you—and sit down, button up your lip and do nothing.' "[16]

David said his soul waited for God more than the watchmen waited for the morning. To be a watchman in his day was a great responsibility, but most of the time you really couldn't do anything. You had to be alert, intensely peering into the darkness to warn the people of imminent danger, but night after night you had only the monotony of the moon to accompany you.

God may require us to watch and wait for what seems like an eternity, but when He acts, He can do more in an instant than we could ever have accomplished had we pursued our own paths. He promises to bring solutions beyond imagination: "For from days of old they have not heard or perceived by ear, nor has the eye seen a God besides you, who acts in behalf of the one who waits for Him" (Isaiah 64:4).

Trusting in our God who never leaves or forsakes us, we watch and wait. "My presence will go with you and I will give you rest" (Exodus 33:14) is the only truth we can cling to at times, but it is enough. Our precious Redeemer longs to comfort and quiet our anxious souls with this reality.

Deep Calls to Deep

The words "deep calls to deep at the sound of Thy waterfalls" were penned by David, perhaps as he fled for his life from his own son Absalom.[17] Alone, afraid, and terribly distraught, we can imagine him stopping to rest near a brook, the hum of a waterfall's roar in the distance. As a deer lopes gracefully by him, pausing at the water's edge to drink, David feels a poignant yearning within and writes, "As the deer pants for the water brooks, so my soul pants for Thee, O God. My soul thirsts for God, for the living God; when shall I come and appear before God? My tears have been my food day and night"(Psalm 42:1–3).

Remembering a time when things were better and God's presence so much more real causes deep depression to well up from the depths of his being. David cries out, "O my God, my soul is in despair within me . . . deep calls to deep at the sound of Thy waterfalls, all Thy breakers and Thy waves have rolled over me" (Psalm 42:6–7).

David felt as if his afflictions had come from the very hand of the God He loved so well. Perhaps you can relate to his distress. There are surely those times for each of us when it seems as if God himself is tossing us about, rolling over us in both small bothersome breakers and great overwhelming waves. How do we keep a quiet heart then?

In the mountainous corridor where I discovered my own wonderful waterfall, the cliffs on either side of the creek jutted out above the trail, forcing me at times to duck under them as I walked. At one point a brass marker explained why. "The overhanging cliff ahead is made of limestone. It is a part of a mountain and should last forever. But even now the creek is eating away at the base. One day it will fall and be washed away. There is no rock that can withstand the power of water."

And so it is. The fact that the infinitely perfect God of the universe draws us into himself can be at once tantalizing and terrifying. One day we may long to escape and another find ourselves thrashing about in the current, yet in the end we know that He is sovereign—there is nothing we can do to withstand His power. But He is also good and loves us with an everlasting love. Quietness comes as we learn to lean into Him, clinging with all our might as His billows roll over us and our soul cries out, "Hope in God, for I shall again praise Him for the help of His presence" (Psalm 42:11).

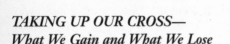

TAKING UP OUR CROSS—
What We Gain and What We Lose

Unbelief is a poison arrow that can make our walk with God miserable and even drive us from His side. Though He does not want us to deny our doubts, if we insist on understanding what He is doing or why, we will not be able to receive the things that He has promised, such as His comfort during affliction or His strength in our weakness. But if we believe that what He says is true, we will seek Him diligently, rejoicing that He longs to personally reward us.

Gain Faith
"And without faith it is impossible to please Him, for he who comes to God must believe that He is, and that He is a rewarder of those who seek Him" (Hebrews 11:6).

Lose Unbelief
"Take care, brethren, that there not be in any one of you an evil, unbelieving heart that falls away from the living God" (Hebrews 3:12).

No human being is immune to the trouble life brings. When we fail to embrace the truth of a sovereign Deity, we end up living "under the circumstances" instead of in His arms. Peace eludes us, for fear lurks behind every situation we face. This is surely an unpleasant way to live. If, however, we bring our fears continually to Christ, He will bear them for us. Only then can the peace of God permeate our days and nights.

Gain Peace

"In peace I will both lie down and sleep, for you alone, O Lord, make me to dwell in safety" (Psalm 4:8).

"Peace I leave with you; My peace I give to you; not as the world gives do I give to you. Do not let your heart be troubled, nor let it be fearful" (John 14:27).

Lose Fear

"You will not be afraid of the terror by night, or of the arrow that flies by day; of the pestilence that stalks in darkness, or of the destruction that lays waste at noon. A thousand may fall at your side and ten thousand at your right hand, but it shall not approach you" (Psalm 91:6–7).

There is great relief in learning to humble ourselves before God when we don't understand His plans. Life is uncertain and changes continually, and only our unchanging God can be relied upon. When we resist Him, anguish is inevitable. But as we take up our cross against the fleshly need to know all things and control our own destiny, we begin to experience a profound stillness, a quiet composure that even the disturbed who cross our paths will long to emulate.

Gain Stillness

"O Lord, my heart is not proud, nor my eyes haughty; nor do I involve myself in great matters, or in things too difficult for me. Surely I have composed and quieted my soul; like a weaned child rests against his mother, My soul is like a weaned child within me" (Psalm 131:1–2).

Lose Anguish

"Distress and anguish terrify him, they overpower him like a king ready for the attack, because he has stretched out his hand against God and conducts himself arrogantly against the Almighty" (Job 15:24–25).

God never intended for His children to carry the weight of the world on their shoulders. We are ill equipped to do so, and the burden of it can only crush us. It is a mystery of faith that in letting go we find rest by clinging to the One who holds not only the worlds but also all the pieces of our life in His loving hands. This is the supreme lifeline for a burdened heart.

Gain Rest

"Come to Me, all who are weary and heavy-laden, and I will give you rest. Take My yoke upon you and learn from Me, for I am gentle and humble in heart, and you will find rest for your souls. For My yoke is easy and My burden is light" (Matthew 11:28–30).

Lose Heavy Burdens

"Casting all your anxiety on Him, because He cares for you" (1 Peter 5:7).

"Cast your burden upon the Lord and He will sustain you; He will never allow the righteous to be shaken" (Psalm 55:22).

Often we act as if we just can't help fretting over the future. But God sees it so very differently. He longs for us to trust in Him and promises that when we do, He will guide us in ways that bring healing and refreshment. Every season of anxiety becomes an opportunity to rejoice in His eternal power and wisdom. When we insist on leaning on our own understanding, bitterness eats away at our resolve, until like senseless, ignorant beasts, we have nowhere to run.

Gain Trust

"Trust in the Lord with all your heart, and do not lean on your own understanding. In all your ways acknowledge Him, and He will make your paths straight. Do not be wise in your own eyes; fear the Lord and turn away from evil. It will be healing to your body and refreshment to your bones" (Proverbs 3:5–8).

Lose Anxiety

"When my anxious thoughts multiply within me, your consolations delight my soul" (Psalm 94:19).

"When my heart was embittered, and I was pierced within, then I was senseless and ignorant; I was like a beast before you" (Psalm 73:21–22).

If we will take up our cross, putting to death the unbelief, fear, anguish, burden-bearing, and anxiety that plague us in our human desire for control, God will transform us into people of faith, peace, stillness, rest, and abiding trust. We will know what a treasure quietness is and how it is found in the arms of a sovereign and good God.

PRACTICING QUIETNESS—
A Mini-Retreat

When we know with certainty that everything that comes into our lives has passed through God's hand first, we can begin to experience His rest. Even the greatest pain we face finds redemptive meaning when we remember the God of the universe has allowed it. He is sovereign. Therein lies the seed of a quiet heart. This extended time of prayer can be a healing time in bringing perspective to all the priorities of our life, helping us learn how to run to the arms of the only One with the power to heal, sustain, strengthen, and purify us.

Preparing Your Heart

Breathe deeply as you thank God for meeting you here today. Make a conscious effort to let all the things that fill your mind fade away. If you need to, jot things down on a piece of paper for later, then focus your mind on God's presence once again. Read the following verses aloud, slowly, peacefully, and quietly, visualizing yourself as a small child resting in God's arms.

"O Lord, my heart is not proud, nor my eyes haughty; nor do I involve myself in great matters, or in things too difficult for me. Surely I have composed and quieted my soul; like a weaned child rests against his mother, My soul is like a weaned child within me. O _____(place your name here), hope in the Lord from this time forth and forever" (Psalm 131).

Wait in this posture until you experience the peace of God.

Read Psalm 37 all the way through one time. Then, in your prayer journal, make two columns with these headings:

I Will Do and Not Do   God Will Do

Go over verses 1–8, 23–24, and 33–40, listing in the first column the things David says not to do and the things he exhorts us to do. When you have completed this, go back over these, listing in the other column the things David says God will do as we learn to wait and trust in Him.

Write a prayer of response to these glorious truths in your prayer journal.

Contemplating His Presence

No other person in Scripture, or perhaps all of history, suffered with the intensity that Job suffered. The record of his experience is a profound one, and it is no accident that God has included it in the canon of His Word. Some historians believe this took place long before Abraham or Moses and thus may have even been given as an encouragement to them.

Often people groan when they think of Job, wondering how God could ever have let all that happen and why He'd want to preserve the record for us. But in reality, Job was extremely blessed, and his experiences created a vision of God and a faith perhaps unparalleled in recorded history. We can learn much from Job, if we will approach him as a hero with honors and medals any loyal soldier would be proud of.

We have done several meditative exercises up to this point, in which I have guided you in the visualization of God's Word. For this chapter, you will have the opportunity to go on your own journey, using an incredible conversation God and Job had as your guide.

First, read Job chapters 1 and 2 to familiarize yourself with the story. Then, write down all the things about your own life, past or present, that have the potential to keep you from having a quiet heart. These can be major issues of faith or minor irritations of daily life.

Next, consider any fears you have and what life might be like if they were realized (e.g., if your spouse died, you lost your job, etc.). Spend some time writing down how you feel about the possibility of these kinds of things, in an open letter to God.

When you have finished, read Job 40 and 41 in their entirety. As you read, stop and meditate on the questions God poses. Hear Him asking you these questions in light of your own struggles with trust. (This will take some time but can be a powerful experience.)

What does this stir in your heart? How are you drawn to respond? What do you see that might encourage you as you seek to live in the quietness God wants for you?

Responding to His Call

Now read Job's reply in chapter 42:1–6. How will you respond to the reality of God's sovereignty? Spend some time in prayer before Him, then write your own response in your prayer journal.

End your time with thanksgiving for what you know is true about God. If you want some guidance, Psalm 145 details many of His attributes.

Going Forward

In a world characterized by high-paced stress and agitation, we have a unique opportunity to reveal the heart of God to those lost without Him. Surely in this day and time, we who are peaceful in the midst of troubling circumstances can be an anomaly that draws others in. As we walk with God, depending on His presence to quiet our own hearts, we will be ever aware of the neediness of those who have no recourse. Let us go toward them with the gentleness we have received.

Notes

1. Harold Rogers, *A Handful of Quietness* (Waco, Tex.: Word Books, 1977), 20.
2. Harold Myra, *Living by God's Surprises* (Waco, Tex.: Word Books, 1988), 22.
3. A. W. Tozer, *The Knowledge of the Holy* (New York: Harper & Row, 1961), 84.
4. Tozer, 110.
5. Curtis and Eldredge, 70–71.
6. Mother Teresa, *Total Surrender* (Ann Arbor, Mich.: Servant Publications, 1985), 38.
7. Horatius Bonar, *Do You Rejoice in God's Sovereignty?* http://grace-for-today.com/bonar.htm.
8. M. Scott Peck, *The Road Less Traveled* (New York: Simon & Schuster, 1978), 15.
9. Madame Jeanne Guyon, *Guyon Speaks Again* (Beaumont, Tex.: Christian Books Publishing House, 1989), 47–48.
10. Myra, 45.
11. Mother Teresa, 37.
12. This story is detailed in Elizabeth Elliot, *Through Gates of Splendor* (Wheaton, Ill.: Tyndale House, 1981).
13. Steve Saint, "Did They Have to Die?," *Christianity Today* magazine (1996): 40:10, 20.
14. W. Bingham Hunter, *The God Who Hears* (Downers Grove, Ill.: InterVarsity Press, 1986), 85.
15. Eugene Peterson, *A Long Obedience in the Same Direction* (Downers Grove, Ill.: InterVarsity Press, 1980), 153.

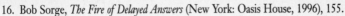

16. Bob Sorge, *The Fire of Delayed Answers* (New York: Oasis House, 1996), 155.
17. There is debate as to the authorship of Psalm 42, but I tend to agree with Spurgeon, who wrote that "it smells of the son of Jesse, it bears the marks of his style and experience in every letter."

CHAPTER SIX

GENTLENESS

Nothing is so strong as gentleness: nothing so gentle as real strength.
Frances de Sales

The legendary musical *Les Misérables*, based on Victor Hugo's novel of nineteenth-century France, tells the story of Jean Valjean, a thief recently released from prison after nineteen years on the chain gang. Because he is required to display a yellow ticket declaring his parolee status wherever he goes, Jean quickly finds he cannot make a fresh start. Battered by the cruelty of a society that will not welcome him into its fold, his last glimmer of hope dissolves, filling him with bitterness.

One night a local bishop discovers him shivering on a bench and invites him in for a warm meal and bed. Jean accepts, but once the bishop falls asleep, he steals some silver and flees. Within minutes he is caught by the police, who do not believe him when he says the silver was a gift.

Dragging him back to the rectory, they are astounded as the bishop affirms that he did indeed give Jean the silver. Turning to the frightened thief, the bishop asks Jean why he left so early, forgetting to take the candlesticks as well. The police have no choice but to release Jean, who is confused by the bishop's kindness. Tenderly the bishop speaks words of gentle encouragement, then sends him off with the bag of silver.

Jean's heart, hardened from years of prison savagery, begins to soften as he ponders the bishop's words:

He treated me like any other.
He gave me his trust,
he called me brother.
My life he claims for God above—
can such things be?
For I had come to hate the world—
this world that always hated me.[1]

In one act of mercy, the bishop empowered Jean to change, and the sphere of his existence would never be the same.

Gentleness is an amazing virtue, for it has the capacity to transform. David, perhaps the most dynamic king in history, knew this well. He declared that divine gentleness enlarged him and made him great (Psalm 18:35). When Jesus called for the weary and heavy laden to come and rest, He invited them to learn from Him, because He was "gentle and humble in heart" (Matthew 11:29).

This flies in the face of a society that adheres to the Darwinian mantra of survival of the fittest. Our dog-eat-dog world can be a desperate place, binding people by the sum of their encounters with it. Victor Hugo, in the original *Les Misérables,* wrote that men were "souls that, crablike, crawl continually toward darkness, going backward in life rather than advancing, using their experience to increase their deformity, growing continually worse, and becoming steeped more and more thoroughly in the intensifying viciousness."[2]

Into such misery our King came, "gentle, and mounted on a donkey" (Matthew 21:5). For those of us who know His tender mercies, the call is clear—freely we have received, freely we must give.

GENTLENESS

A kind and compassionate disposition that emanates from those
who have experienced the tender mercies of God.

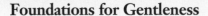

Foundations for Gentleness

Some of the harshest Christians are those who have known the Lord the longest or are the most biblically literate. Why is this? If gentleness is a fruit of the Holy Spirit who dwells within, then shouldn't this quality increase as we mature in our faith? It should but often doesn't. What must we do when gentleness seems to elude us? How do we guard ourselves against cynical self-righteousness as we live in a world of fallen people? The key is in coming to terms with our own neediness—to learn to live by the deep conviction that *there but for the grace of God go I.*

Our Sin Incites the Wrath of God

God's wrath is not a pleasant or easy subject. For me, it conjures up memories of childhood preachers ranting about hell and the horrors of unending fire. Perhaps you struggle with it as well. Though the hellfire-and-damnation thrust of the past was certainly out of balance, it seems our tendency today is to ignore God's wrath altogether or relegate it to abstract discussions of the lost and eternity.

But because Scripture refers to God's wrath so often, we must seek to understand its significance for our lives as believers today. And while it may seem incongruous to speak of God's wrath in a discussion on gentleness, seeing the raw reality of our own condition before a righteous God may become the impetus for us to develop the hearts of compassion we need.

The word translated "wrath" in Scripture refers to "heat, poison, and venom" and always denotes a strong emotional state of anger.[3] For example, Moses told the Israelites that he feared the anger and hot displeasure with which the Lord was wrathful against them (Deuteronomy 9:19). The prophets of the Old Testament had often warned the Israelites of God's impending judgment, using the metaphor of a cup. Isaiah called it the chalice of reeling (Isaiah 51:17). Over and over, God poured it out like boiling venom when His people rebelled (Psalm 75:8).

The wrath of God is not arbitrary—it is forceful and direct. A holy God cannot help but respond with extreme anger in the face of sin. The entire character of God would be in question if in His infinite perfection, hearts that rebel or respond to Him with indifference did not insult Him.

God demonstrates His wrath no more grievously than in the death of His own Son, Jesus Christ. One dark night in a garden called Gethsemane, Christ fell to His face crying out, "Abba! Father! All things are possible for You; remove this cup from Me; yet not what I will, but what You will" (Mark 14:36).

Jesus Christ drank the eternal cup of God's wrath against our sin when He gave His life on Calvary. Every slap to His face, every drop of spittle on His neck, every flick of the flagellum against His mangled back, every thud of the hammer on the nails through His hands and feet bear testimony to the gravity of almighty God's righteous indignation against sin.

Oh, that we had spiritual eyes to see this. Jesus paid a terrible price for a people who would have otherwise known only the wrath of His Father. The heaviness of this should settle on us until overwhelmed with gratitude we cry out, *Thank You, O precious Redeemer, for in Your wrath You have remembered mercy!* (Habakkuk 3:2).

Our Salvation Requires the Mercy of God

As difficult and troubling as it may be, seeing the breadth of God's wrath is a blessing, for it enables us to truly plumb the depths of His mercy. How precious is this facet of our Lord's character. The concept of mercy in Scripture encompasses many things. It refers to bending or stooping in kindness to an inferior being, feeling deep compassion, watchful tenderness (such as a mother caring for the child in her womb), and an attitude of pity that manifests itself in outward action.[4]

God is merciful. Therefore, He cares deeply about the misery we bring upon ourselves when we sin. Because He knows our frailty and feels compassion for our hopeless estate, He has pity, stooping down in kindness to take action that can relieve our pain. Scripture says God delights in showing mercy to His people (Micah 7:18).

In the Old Testament, God promised the Israelites that if they loved Him and kept His commandments, His mercy toward them would endure for a thousand generations (Deuteronomy 7:9). Amazingly, even when Israel broke their side of the agreement, God kept His. He spoke through Jeremiah that though they had disobeyed, His heart would not let Him forget them. " 'Indeed, as often as I have spoken against him, I certainly still remember him; therefore My heart yearns for him; I will surely have mercy on him,' declares the Lord" (Jeremiah 31:20).

Jesus' death not only demonstrated the extent of God's wrath but it was also the ultimate exhibition of the merciful heart of our Father. When Zechariah saw the infant Christ in the temple, He prophesied that He would bring salvation through forgiveness of sins because of God's tender mercy (Luke 1:77–78).

Our salvation is completely dependent on a God who not only loves us but is also motivated from the depths of His nature to rescue us from His wrath. He does not give us what we deserve, having made provision for punishment through the death of His Son (Ephesians 2:1–5). How we must rejoice that "He saved us, not on the basis of deeds which we have done in righteousness, but according to His mercy" (Titus 3:5).

Our Need Evokes the Gentleness of God

Scripture is replete with metaphors for the gentleness with which God makes overtures toward us. He likens himself to an eagle that finds the Israelites—an abandoned nest of baby chicks—dying in the howling waste of wilderness. There He encircles and cares for them, guarding them as He would the pupil of His eye, hovering over them, carrying them, catching them when they fall (Deuteronomy 32:10–11).

One day as Jesus approached Jerusalem, He looked out and lamented that He was like a mother hen watching a bird of prey approaching her chicks, longing to gather them under her wings to keep them from harm (Luke 13:34). On another occasion, He simply stopped and wept at their neediness (Luke 19:41).

Perhaps the most comforting portrayal of God's gentleness is as Shepherd of our souls. He finds us when we are scattered, lost and going our own way, and with great rejoicing carries us into the fold of His eternal embrace. Jesus, the Good Shepherd, who lays down His life for the sheep, is also the door by which we enter the safety of God's presence. This metaphor has profound significance, as one shepherd demonstrates:

> Each sheep is inspected with great care. Many of them have been bruised by the sharp-edged rocks, or their flesh has been torn by the briars, and with the olive oil and cedar-tar the bruises are treated. But to the tired, worn, and weary one of the flock, whose face and head are bathed with the oil, the shepherd also gives needed refreshment.[5]

Only one thing about us evokes this kind of tenderness from an omnipotent God—our desperate need. He is not drawn to our abilities, our talents, our accomplishments, our goals, or our commitments. His heart is stirred when we are broken, and He reaches for us in our frailty, for He knows full well our helpless condition. Jesus was anointed by God to preach the Good News to the poor, offer release to the captives, give sight to the blind, and heal the oppressed (Luke 4:18).

We must cling to the profound mystery that our weakness and not our strength evokes the gentleness of God. This truth has the potential to alter every encounter we have with others on this earth, for when we see it, we can only relate in ways that reflect a keen awareness of our own deficiency. How we must cry out to God to reveal our neediness so we might learn from our Savior who is gentle and humble in heart.

Barriers to Gentleness

The life of Matthew Shepard, a twenty-two-year-old political science major at the University of Wyoming, was brutally snuffed out one night by two young men who robbed him, tied him to a fence, then beat him and burned him as he begged them to stop. News accounts indicated that though robbery was the motive, the men knew Matthew was homosexual and made derogatory remarks about it after the killing. As the nation took sides over the political issues of hate crimes and gay rights, Matthew's parents pleaded for the world to let them mourn the death of their only son in peace.

Two churches refused. From Kansas and Texas they came, protesting Matthew's lifestyle while friends and family grieved his death. Holding signs that read: *Remember Lot's wife, No fags in heaven,* and *God hates fags,* some spewed angry and vengeful epithets at the funeral attendees.

The church of Jesus Christ today is often portrayed by the media as angry, narrow, mean-spirited, and lacking compassion. Though these kinds of actions may be rare and extreme, we all bear the consequences and should seek to find ways to counteract negative stereotypes. We simply are not by and large a people known for merciful hearts or gentle hands. Thus we must look hard at those things that keep us from extending the gentle love of Christ to a broken world.

We Misunderstand God's Mercy

In *Les Misérables,* the scene following Jean's encounter with the bishop takes place eight years later. Having assumed a new identity, the former prisoner has now become both mayor and factory owner in a distant town, where he is known by his love for the poor and kindness to the downtrodden. Unbeknownst to Jean, his new police chief Javert was one of his former prison guards and has spent the past eight years pursuing him for breaking parole. At first, Javert does not recognize Jean, but soon something happens to stir his memory and he becomes bitterly determined to bring the convict-turned-upstanding-citizen down. Jean is forced to flee the community he has come to love, with Javert following close on his tail.

The rest of the musical tells the story of these two men whose lives are now painfully intertwined. Javert is a tragic arch villain with an obsession to see Jean Valjean pay for breaking the law. Jean, ever aware of the gift of grace given him by the bishop, lives to bless others, even while on the run. When through a series of events Jean finds the tables turned and has the opportunity to kill Javert, he decides instead to let him go, though it means he must flee once again for his own life.

Some nights later Javert, filled with resentment that Jean is free again, vows to continue the hunt until he destroys him completely. He sings:

> *There, out in the darkness,*
> *a fugitive running, fallen from grace.*
> *God be my witness, I never shall yield*
> *till we come face to face. . . .*
> *And so it must be, and so it is written*
> *on the doorway to Paradise.*
> *That those who falter and those who fail*
> *must pay the price.*[6]

Javert, like many, never grasped the reality that his own rigid adherence to the law had not secured God's favor nor had it made him immune to God's wrath. He could not see that even at his best, he was a sinner with no way out. For every one of us the truth remains, there is a price on our heads, and if we had to pay it we would be destroyed, because we simply cannot.

This is what makes God's mercy so very precious to our hearts. Who *can* receive it? What makes it accessible to any of us? Though we may never understand the mystery of election, Scripture is clear that God grants mercy as He pleases. He reminds us through the apostle Paul: "I will have mercy on whom I have mercy, and I will have compassion on whom I have compassion." Driving the point home further, Paul adds, "So then, it does not depend on the man who wills or the man who runs, but on God who has mercy" (Romans 9:14–16).

How incredible to be God's chosen beloved, to be beneficiaries of His mercy through no merit of our own. When this reality takes root within us, we will be awestruck by it. No longer will we boast or see ourselves as superior to others, nor will we act as if our own righteousness were anything but a gift from God (1 Corinthians 4:7). Every relationship we have will reflect the understanding that "we are all equally privileged but unentitled beggars at the door of God's mercy."[7] Then, instead of weighing people down with burdens too hard to bear, like the Pharisees did (Luke 11:46), we'll hold out open arms, gently calling them to join us at the foot of the Cross, where the ground is truly level.

We Are Not Experiencing God's Mercy for Ourselves

The experience of God's mercy is not academic. It cannot be contained within the comfortable framework of dogma most of us embrace. It is explosive, extravagant, gut-wrenching, consuming, and even offensive. God drenches us with His mercy only when the pain of our neediness erupts in a cry: "God, be merciful to me, a sinner!"

Some of us have either never understood this or have moved too quickly past it. We settle for an intellectual grasp, our security neatly packaged in the theology of redemption. But from the souls of those who have come to grips with God's kindness in the face of their unworthiness, a sense of wonder resonates. It's almost like being moment by moment pleasantly surprised that God isn't giving up on us.

I confess there are times, perhaps more often than not, that I take God's mercy for granted. I tend to relate more with the Pharisees, who prided themselves in their status before God as they diligently kept the law, than with the prostitutes and beggars, the mentally ill, and the crooked businessmen Jesus was drawn to. Recently I read the story of the immoral woman who anointed Jesus' feet, and in all honesty I saw myself clearly in the things Simon the Pharisee, in whose house Jesus was eating, said and did.

As a Pharisee well versed in the Torah, Simon knew volumes about the mercy of God. Three times a day he joined all orthodox Jews in reciting Psalm 136, a veritable smorgasbord of God's merciful acts. But when this woman of the street burst through the door, breaking every possible law of Jewish etiquette, Simon was incensed. I can imagine him thinking that he'd only invited the itinerant preacher named Yeshua to lunch to see what all the fuss was about, since he'd supposedly healed the blind and even raised the dead. But now, watching this woman fall all over him was disgusting. *Didn't he know what kind of tramp was kissing his feet? Why didn't her outrageous display of emotionalism bother him? What kind of Jew was he anyway?*

Jesus knew what Simon was thinking and responded by telling him a story of two debtors—one owing much and one owing little. Then He asked Simon which debtor would love the moneylender more if both were forgiven their debts. Simon replied, "I suppose the one whom he forgave more." In agreement, Jesus went on:

> Do you see this woman? I entered your house; you gave Me no water for My feet, but she has wet My feet with her tears and wiped them with her hair. You gave Me no kiss; but she, since the time I came in, has not ceased to kiss My feet. You did not anoint My head with oil, but she anointed My feet with perfume. For this reason I say to you, her sins, which are many, have been forgiven, for she loved much; but he who is forgiven little, loves little. (Luke 7:44–47)

The immoral woman possessed something far more valuable than all Simon's knowledge *about* God's mercy—she lived in the experience of it. Simon, having no sense of his own indebtedness, viewed her with contempt instead of being astounded at the wonder of God's unconditional love for himself *and* her.

When we find ourselves failing to extend gentleness toward others, perhaps it is because we do not abide in the shadow of the Cross, reminiscing regularly on what we were or might have been without it. Paul told Titus we must be gentle with each other, remembering we once were "foolish, disobedient, deceived, enslaved to lusts and pleasures, spending our lives in malice and envy, hateful and hating one another" (Titus 3:1–3).

The degree of gentleness we extend flows from the measure of mercy we experience daily in our heart of hearts. How we need to revel in God's tender love for our impoverished souls, swimming in the streams of His mercy. Only then can we view God's creatures as He does. Only then can we live out Christ's maxim to have mercy on them in the same way He has had mercy on us (Luke 7:33). For many of us this barrier to gentleness stands strong.

We Expect Everyone to Walk at Our Pace

In the book of Genesis, after Jacob and Esau were emotionally reunited and their relationship restored, Esau invited Jacob's family to return to Seir with him. Jacob responded that the children were frail and there were flocks and herds to nurse. Not willing to drive them in ways that might destroy them, he asked Esau, "Please let my Lord pass on before his servant, and I will proceed at my leisure, according to the pace of the cattle that are before me and according to the pace of the children, until I come to my Lord at Seir" (Genesis 33:13–14).

What a beautiful example for the body of Christ. God calls us to walk side by side, sometimes slowing down to hold another up. When we force those younger, less mature, less knowledgeable, or less spiritually astute to walk at our pace, the results can be devastating.

As young missionaries in the Alaskan bush, my husband and I learned this lesson in a compelling way. Due to a series of tragic circumstances, I found myself close to a nervous breakdown, not knowing if I could go on. In despair, we flew to share with our supervisor what was happening and to break the news that we thought we might need to leave our mission work for good.

Don Rollins, a veteran Alaskan missionary, was a trailblazer whose years of service in the bush had earned him the reputation of *legend*. The village we served in was dear to his heart, and our coming had been the culmination of years of planning and praying on his part. Fully expecting him to remind us of our call, our commitment, the cost to the mission board, and the condition of lost Eskimos, I was taken aback by his response.

Gently, he related that the work there was not dependent on us—that what mattered most right then was our welfare. As he assured us that we had a lifetime of ministry in which God desired to use us, I felt an enormous weight lift from my shoulders. Somehow his freeing us up to leave empowered us to stay. That day we went back to our village, where God did a great work both among the people and in our hearts over the course of our assignment there.

I've thought a lot about the risk Don took that day. If he hadn't, I'm not sure we'd be celebrating almost twenty-five years of full-time Christian ministry. He did not demand that we walk at his pace, although surely he had the right to. This is the kind of gentleness we need more of in the body of Christ today.

What We Must Do

How my heart grieves for battered-down souls both within the church and without. Where is the refuge, the shelter from the inevitable storms of life in a fallen world? Where can the afflicted hear good news and the wounds of the brokenhearted be bound? When will we become a people who set others free by proclaiming God's favor instead of projecting our judgment (Isaiah 61:1–2)?

Today the Shepherd of our souls calls for a gentleness that will draw others in rather than make them shrink back in shame or fear. What can we do to see this become a reality? I believe there are three actions on our part that enable God to increase the fruit of gentleness in our lives.

Regularly Acknowledge Our Condition Before God

A popular bumper sticker reads, "Christians aren't perfect, just forgiven." While the words reflect truth, it has always made me a little uncomfortable, perhaps because it seems to smack of a certain smugness. The reality of our redeemed status isn't something to flaunt like a victory banner in the faces of those who have not received God's grace. Rather, it should cause us to live quietly, tenderly, and humbly in the arms of the living God who has had mercy on us.

If I desire to be gentle with others, I must reflect often on the sobering truth that I too was a lamb gone astray, that my sin nailed Jesus to the cross. I can never forget that the very best I had to offer God—my most valiant attempts to be good, do right, and please Him—were old rags, the stench of which could only repel Him (Isaiah 53:6; 64:6).

The Lord has shown me that by comparing myself to others, I can be easily deceived about my own unworthiness. God warns us not to do this, saying, "Stop regarding man, whose breath of life is in his nostrils; for why should he be esteemed?" (Isaiah 2:22). By the world's standards, I might look pretty good. But our standard is not the world, or even the church, but the righteousness of a perfect God. "Pretty good" under the spotlight of His holiness is not much to look at. In fact, not only is pretty good not good enough, without God's mercy it would earn me the eternal torment of hell.

As long as I have the least illusion that I deserve anything God has done for me, I will expect others to prove their worth as well, binding them with expectations they can never meet. But when I see myself as God does—in grave need of the mercy He freely bestows and unable to do anything to earn it—I will reach out in gentleness to those who share my impoverished condition.

Speak the Truth in Love

To be gentle with one another does not mean to ignore sin, weakness, or harmful behavior. Often the most merciful thing we can do is to speak of one's shortcomings with them. We are all blinded by sin and need to be iron sharpening iron in each other's lives (Proverbs 27:17). This has always been God's plan for the body of Christ.

But gentleness must permeate our hearts and flow through our words if our goal is to see people become what God has called them to be. In Galatians 6:1, Paul admonishes us to restore each other in a spirit of gentleness. The word for "restore" is the same one used to refer to "mending a net" or "setting a broken bone." It is a slow, at times tedious, process and can't be done with reckless abandon. We must not "destroy good grain among the weeds by trying to weed too quickly!"[8]

We are to speak the truth in love. If we cannot extend the same unconditional, sacrificial, *agape* love that Jesus demonstrated on the cross, then we are not ready to speak at all and must wait until God changes our heart (Ephesians 4:14–15). When He purifies our souls, deep love for the brethren will result (1 Peter 1:22). Only then will we be able "to strengthen the hands that are weak and the knees that are feeble, and make straight paths for their feet, so that the limb which is lame may not be put out of joint, but rather be healed" (Hebrews 12:12–13).

Look for Ways to Demonstrate Gentleness

On any given day we have many occasions to demonstrate the gentleness of Christ. It might be as simple as a kind word or a tender pat on the back. As parents, we can be patient with our children's weaknesses, for we remember our own. With kindness, we can teach them the joy of living in the security of Christ's love. As spouses, how free we would be to grow in love for each other if we covered all our words and deeds with a cloak of gentleness.

We live in a terribly needy world—the broken, abused, downtrodden, distraught, and confused confront us at every turn. It is easy to throw up our hands, feeling we can't possibly make a difference. But we can, for the Spirit of our merciful Father lives within us and wants to glorify himself through our acts of kindness toward others (Isaiah 61:10–11; Matthew 5:16).

If we aren't intentional about this, we will probably miss out on opportunities right before our eyes. In the story of the good Samaritan, both a priest and a Levite passed by the wounded man, but the Samaritan saw him and, feeling compassion, went to bind his wounds. Clearly our religious status or even spiritual zeal does not ensure that we will see the needy in our path.

Mother Teresa told how one day as a young woman she came upon a dying leper, and before she had time to evaluate the situation, she'd taken the old woman home with her. That was a defining moment for this nun who impacted the world with the love of Christ perhaps more profoundly than anyone else in the twentieth century. She wrote in her later years:

> I never look at the masses as my responsibility. I look only at the individual. I can love only one person at a time. I can feed only one person at a time. Just one, one, one. So you begin . . . I begin. I picked up one person—maybe if I didn't pick up that one person I wouldn't have picked up the others. The whole work is only a drop in the ocean. But if we don't put the drop in, the ocean would be one drop less. Same thing for you. Same thing in your family. Same thing in the church where you go. Just begin . . . one, one, one . . .[9]

Gentleness—a Gift to the World and to Ourselves

Les Misérables comes to a climax in a final confrontation between the two men. Jean is emerging from an underground sewer where he has been trapped with his daughter's boyfriend, who suffers injuries from fighting in a civil insurrection. Javert awaits, ready to arrest both of them. Jean pleads for time to get the young man to the hospital. Here Javert is faced with the greatest dilemma of his life. His rigid principles of justice demand that he arrest Jean, but he cannot get away from the reality that his own life was spared by this common criminal he has grown to hate so much.

He turns, allowing Jean to escape once again, and then begins to run, torment filling his soul. Finally, he reaches a place where the Seine River is swollen to dangerous levels and, plunging himself into it, kills himself.

Javert had lived all his life by an external standard that fed the bitter cancer within his soul and in the end felt such agony he was compelled to take his own life. Some surmise he simply could not come to terms with the kindness of another's merciful act, while others suggest that because his principles required a price to be paid, when he let Jean go, his own death became the only possible solution.

Les Misérables is a tale of two very different lives. Jean Valjean lived by grace, while Javert lived by the law. Jean knew his sin, while Javert relished his piety. Jean extended mercy to others, while Javert demanded justice. In the end, Jean and Javert died two very different deaths.

Jean Valjean, having been set free by the bishop's simple act of mercy, lived the rest of his days reaching out to those less fortunate than himself. His life was punctuated by mercy and permeated with love. All who came in contact with him were changed by his gentleness. Yet he saw himself as the one enriched and in the end proclaimed his joy was a debt he owed those he'd helped. Dying, he reached out to those he had loved, singing, "And remember the truth that once was spoken. To love another person is to see the face of God!"[10]

Valjean's dying words reflect the amazing mystery that in extending tender love to others we experience for ourselves the manifest presence of a merciful God. "Truly I say to you, to the extent that you did it to one of these brothers of Mine, even the least of them, you did it to Me" (Matthew 25:40). What a blessed cycle of mercy Christ has purposed for our lives. We cannot fail unless the cycle stops with us, for then we become reservoirs in which God's streams of mercy stagnate, and we ourselves lose the gift.

Let us be continually drawn by the gentle Shepherd to receive mercy in our own time of need. Then, compelled by the compassion we've received, we will live in the joy of being channels of gentleness to a very needy world.

✑   ✑

TAKING UP OUR CROSS—
What We Gain and What We Lose

Gentleness creates an atmosphere of freedom in the church and kindness as we go out. The crucified Christian believes Christ died for sinners and is therefore intent on crossing every barrier, breaking down every wall, as an agent of God's mercy. As partiality, prejudice, apathy, and abrasive attitudes are put to death, we pursue the lost, for our deepest desire is to see them experience the saving mercy of Christ.

Gain Compassion

"To the weak I became weak, that I might win the weak; I have become all things to all men, so that I may by all means save some" (1 Corinthians 9:22).

"For though I am free from all men I have made myself a slave to all, so that I may win more" (1 Corinthians 9:19).

Lose Intolerance

"The Lord's bond-servant must not be quarrelsome, but be kind to all, able to teach, patient when wronged, with gentleness correcting those who are in opposition, if perhaps God may grant them repentance leading to the knowledge of the truth" (2 Timothy 2:24–25).

Gentle people are peaceable—not given to quick outbursts of anger or combative spirits. Instead, they know the art of quiet reason, often convincing others of truth more with the integrity of their lives than the cleverness of their words.

Gain Reasonableness

"Who among you is wise and understanding? Let him show by his good behavior his deeds in the gentleness of wisdom. . . . But the wisdom from above is first pure, then peaceable, gentle, reasonable, full of mercy and good fruits, unwavering, without hypocrisy" (James 3:13, 17).

Lose Quick Temper

"What is the source of quarrels and conflicts among you? Is not the source your pleasures that wage war in your members?" (James 4:1).

"A gentle answer turns away wrath, but a harsh word stirs up anger" (Proverbs 15:1).

God desires to use the members of His body to help one another change and grow. But when we cling to selfish agendas, we become impatient, wanting our way more than we want to help others mature. To be gentle is to be patient in the face of others' weaknesses, ignorance, or failures, even when they cause discomfort or suffering in our own lives, for this is pleasing to God.

Gain Patience

"For every high priest taken from among men . . . can deal gently with the ignorant and misguided, since he himself also is beset with weakness" (Hebrews 5:1–2).

"A man's discretion makes him slow to anger, and it is his glory to overlook a transgression" (Proverbs 19:11).

Lose Impatience

"We urge you, brethren, admonish the unruly, encourage the fainthearted, help the weak, be patient with everyone" (1 Thessalonians 5:14).

"For what credit is there if, when you sin and are harshly treated, you endure it with patience? But if when you do what is right and suffer for it you patiently endure it, this finds favor with God" (1 Peter 2:20).

If it required God's kindness to lead us to repentance (Romans 2:4), then surely He wants us to be vessels of kindness to others. To do so, we must die to harsh judgment, haughty criticism, and arrogant condemnation. Instead, gently upholding our brothers and sisters, we lead the broken, the fallen, the discouraged, and the lost to the comfort of our Savior's side.

Gain Kindness

"But love your enemies, and do good, and lend, expecting nothing in return; and your reward will be great, and you will be sons of the Most High; for He Himself is kind to ungrateful and evil men" (Luke 6:35).

Lose Harshness

"Let all bitterness and wrath and anger and clamor and slander be put away from you, along with all malice. Be kind to one another, tender-hearted, forgiving each other, just as God in Christ also has forgiven you" (Ephesians 4:31–32).

There is no greater call than that which Christ Jesus gave in His final hours for unity. He promised this would provide incontrovertible proof that He was who He said He was. Unity is only possible as we lay down our rights, our individualism, and our independence, gently receiving each other in our diligent pursuit of the bond of peace.

Gain Unity

"Therefore, I, the prisoner of the Lord, implore you to walk in a manner worthy of the calling with which you have been called, with all humility and gentleness, with patience, showing tolerance for one another in love, being diligent to preserve the unity of the Spirit in the bond of peace" (Ephesians 4:1–3).

Lose Disunity

"Who among you is wise and understanding? Let him show by his good behavior his deeds in the gentleness of wisdom. But if you have bitter jealousy and selfish ambition in your heart, do not be arrogant and so lie against the truth" (James 3:13–14).

Oh, how the church of Jesus Christ would flourish if we willingly died to intolerance, impatience, harshness, quick tempers, and disunity, for when we do, our Shepherd fills us with compassion, patience, kindness, reasonableness, and unity. Then, as individuals growing in the warmth of a nurturing family, we can hold out to the world the hope our gentle Savior has instilled within each of us.

⟠　　　⟠

PRACTICING GENTLENESS—
A Mini-Retreat

Gentleness means we not only see the needs of those around us but we are also compelled to reach out to them. This is not something we can conjure up or even clarify by steps. The most effective way to bring about a spirit of gentleness in our own lives is not by doing but by being. We are filled with the gentleness of Christ as we learn to live in the warmth of His tender mercies toward us.

Our confidence is truly found in the Father heart of God who rejoices over His own Son's kindness to fallen man. Jesus is our supreme example of gentleness. Because He will not break a bruised reed or snuff out a smoldering wick (Isaiah 42:3), He brings His Father great joy. How tenderly He treats us:

When a reed is bent and about to break, the Servant will hold it upright until it heals. When a wick is smoldering and has scarcely any heat left, the Servant will not pinch it off, but cup his hand and blow gently until it burns. Thus the Father cries, "Behold, my Servant in whom my soul delights."[11]

May you experience such tender kindness today.

Preparing Your Heart

Spend a few minutes reflecting on the kindness of God toward you. See your heart as a dry sponge receiving the water of His Spirit to fill you and quench your thirst. Just drink in His presence for a period of time.

Read Psalm 103, first to yourself, contemplating the truths of all that God is and does for you. Then turn it into a praise back to God (e.g., *I will bless you, Lord, from the depths of my soul, everything in me will bless your holy name. I will bless you and forget none of the amazing things you have done for me*).

Write one thing that speaks most to you from this passage as a prayer of thanksgiving in your journal.

Contemplating His Presence

Read Isaiah 53:6, Luke 15:3–7, and Ezekiel 34:11–16. Ask God's Spirit to illuminate His Word and write the heart of it within you.

Keepers of sheep tell us that sheep have a tendency to stubbornly insist on going their own way. When they do, they will follow the same path over and over until it is a useless rut, void of any beauty or sustenance. Yet they will not change direction or look for greener pastures. Even when injured or as death begins to overtake them, they fail to lift their eyes from the devastation beneath their determined feet. Left to their own devices, they would face inevitable destruction.

God had good reason for comparing His people to sheep. Though we have a Good Shepherd who promises abundant life, we often find ourselves shuffling along, determined to find our own way, even at the risk of personal devastation. The rut gets deeper, our commitment to it more entrenched, and we can no longer see beyond our next step.

Offer a prayer to the Lord, telling Him of your own need as a wayward lamb and of the ruts you may be in or the injuries you suffer from right now. You may want to write it in your prayer journal.

When you have finished, read the following visualization a couple of times. Then close your eyes and allow yourself to experience this as if it were happening to you at this moment.

Imagine yourself wandering along a desolate path. You are worn out, barely able to put one foot in front of the other. The air is heavy and there is no sign of life anywhere around. You know this path so well you don't even have to think—you just keep plodding along. Blisters have formed on your feet and some are bleeding. The pain is great.

You long for something better, wishing moment by moment that you could break away from the course your life is taking. But the thought of trying seems overwhelming—it is just so much easier to continue as you have always done. Every bone in your body aches, your stomach is in knots, and anxiety grips your heart. But there appears to be no way out. The abundant life you were promised now seems like a forgotten dream, and while you long to return to the fold of God's comforting presence, you have no idea how to escape from this endless rut.

As you stumble along in frustration, you are startled by a voice. You slow down a little, listening carefully for another sound. There it is—that voice again. It is loving and warm . . . and it is calling your name. Now you come to a complete standstill, afraid to move even the least bit. You long to hear the voice again.

Listen as your name echoes through the air. That voice—drawing you from deep within to be still, to hear, and to respond. As you turn toward the sound of the voice, you see Jesus, the Good Shepherd.

Fearing disapproval or rejection, you turn back to your well-worn path.

But He calls your name again, and as you look back, you see love and great joy in His eyes. He seems almost elated to see you and you cannot imagine why.

Now He is moving toward you. Tenderly He joins you on the path, His soothing touch on your back. Then He turns you toward Him and gently holds your face in His hands, wiping away the tears and sweat. Kneeling down, He washes the wounds on your feet, pouring warm, soothing oil into them. He looks up and smiles at you in a way that melts the hardened corners of your heart. You have never known such comfort as this and you hope against hope that He will never leave.

Then He stands up and looking across the vast horizon begins to sing a beautiful song. He picks you up and, carrying you close to His heart, whirls you around and around and around. Heavenly voices begin to join His in a harmony beyond description. The sound of it fills the entire expanse of the universe. Hear them sing of the glorious Shepherd who with everlasting joy rescues scattered lambs. They tell of your value to Him—though you had gone astray, the Good Shepherd has come to restore your very soul. He's left everything to find you and bring you safely home. Rest in His arms as He carries you rejoicing into the loving fold of His will and purpose for your life.

Wait for a while in God's presence, receiving and relishing in His mercy. Thank Him for not leaving you in the howling waste of wilderness. Praise Him for delivering you from the ruts of your own making. Ask Him to continue to reveal just how lost you are without His tender touch.

Responding to His Call

Write out Isaiah 40:11 and 1 Peter 2:25, placing your name in them. Reflect on the wonder of these truths.

Now picture the people in your life—your family, neighbors, friends, brothers and sisters in Christ. Having received this kind of gentleness from

Christ your Shepherd, what do you long to bring to them? Is there any place for harshness, arrogance, judgment, impatience, or condescension?

According to Colossians 3:12, with what will you clothe yourself as you go toward them? Where can you learn these things and to what lengths should you go to demonstrate them? (Ephesians 5:1–2).

Spend some time in prayer, asking God to show you specific needs for a gentle touch among those you know. As you pray for them, commit to reaching out in kindness.

Finish your time with thanksgiving to the Lord using the following verses: 2 Corinthians 1:3–4; Romans 5:8–9; 1 Thessalonians 5:9–11; and 1 Timothy 1:16.

Going Forward

How incredibly blessed are the chosen of God. To be the recipients of His tender mercies, to feel His gentle Spirit caressing and correcting our souls is surely a benefit beyond compare. What joy fills the heart of the Lord's beloved. This joy may be the most magnificent gain of the crucified life. God's people have always been characterized by this trait more than any other as they submitted their lives to Him. Let us consider this wonderful virtue, discovering that we exist to "joyously draw water from the springs of salvation" (Isaiah 12:3).

Notes

1. "What Have I Done?" from *Les Misérables* by Alain Boublil & Claude Michel Schonberg, lyrics by Herbert Kretzmer, Alain Boublil Music, Ltd. 1985, based on the novel by Victor Hugo, printed at http://memberstr:pod.com/pointll/lmlyric/htm.

2. Victor Hugo, *Les Misérables*, public domain, gopher://wiretap.area.com/00/ Library/Classic/lesmis.vh.

3. *Vine's Expository Dictionary of Biblical Words* (Nashville: Thomas Nelson Publishers, 1985), electronic database, 1996 Biblesoft.

4. *Vincent's Word Studies of the New Testament* and *Vine's Expository Dictionary of Biblical Words*, electronic database, 1996 Biblesoft.

5. Joseph Howard Gray, *The Shepherd God: Meditations on the Twenty-third Psalm* (Philadelphia: Universal Book and Bible House, 1943), 64.

6. "Stars," from *Les Misérables*.

7. Brennan Manning, *The Ragamuffin Gospel* (Portland, Ore.: Multnomah Press, 1990), 23.

8. Madame Jeanne Guyon, *Guyon Speaks Again* (Beaumont, Tex.: Christian Books Publishing House, 1989), 94.

9. Mother Teresa, *Works of Love Are Works of Peace* (San Francisco: Ignatius Press, 1996), 35.

10. "On My Own," from *Les Misérables*.

11. John Piper, *The Pleasures of God* (Portland, Ore.: Multnomah Press, 1991), 26.

CHAPTER SEVEN
JOY

From silly devotions and sour-faced saints, spare us, O Lord.
Teresa of Avila

In their tongue-in-cheek analysis of twentieth-century American evangelicalism, the authors of *Growing Up Born Again* write:

> *Saved. Born again. Redeemed. Converted.* Those of us who grew up in BA families knew that we belonged to a very select body of people. We were special, set apart, chosen. We were real Christians.
>
> Of course, there were a lot of people who said they were Christians, meaning they weren't Hindu or Muslim or Jewish. But we knew we were *real* Christians.
>
> How did we know? Here are some guidelines.[1]

The guidelines included a list of do's and a much longer list of don'ts. For example, a *real* Christian was someone who had not only accepted Jesus as their personal Savior but also believed in the Holy Bible, had been baptized, had daily devotions, and witnessed to the lost. A real Christian was also someone who did *not* go to movies, dance, listen to rock and roll, play cards (except for Rook or Old Maid), gamble, or use dice (except the ones that come with the Monopoly game), and, of course, *never* drank or smoked (except the deacons on the front steps after church).

I relate well, for I too grew up BA—born again. And though there was great emphasis on *accepting Jesus*, equally important were the unwritten rules we were to live by. For me, as well as many others, faith was largely about what we could and couldn't do. That was what made us different; those were the things that set us apart—a message I heard throughout my life.

The death knell has been sounded for a church that focuses more on what we do for God than what He has done for us, though it may be oblivious to the funeral march droning in the distance. The tragic effects are felt both within the body and without. What would ever compel a lost world to embrace a gospel whose adherents are characterized by gritted teeth, laborious service, and self-righteous distance? Where is the joy?

Foundations for Joy

The concept of joy is predominant in Scripture. In the Old Testament alone we are told 155 times to rejoice! The root word for joy includes a spontaneous feeling of jubilance prompted by some external stimulus, a feeling so strong that it must find expression.[2] Thus, to rejoice is to express with unrestrained exuberance our response to God's character, His ways, and His presence among men. The Old Testament word for "joy" carried a literal connotation of *spinning around with pleasure*!

The New Testament word is *chara* meaning "cheerfulness" or "calm delight."[3] Christians should be readily identifiable as those with cheerful demeanors. The delight of *Who* we know should bubble up in us until it spills out, like a secret we can't keep any longer. For this to happen, we must grasp the heritage of joy we've been given, the object and source of our joy, and how God expands our capacity to receive joy.

Man Was Made for Joy

Joy emanated from the heart of God from the moment He spoke the world into being. With each step of creation He paused to enjoy the fruit of His labor, saying, "It is good." Watching the wonder of it all, the morning stars sang and the angels shouted for joy (Job 38:7).

Scripture teaches that all of creation is a testimony to joy. The trees of the forest sing for joy, the dawn and sunset shout for joy, the fields exult, the rivers clap their hands, the mountains sing, and, in fact, the entire earth breaks forth into shouts of joy (1 Chronicles 16:33; Psalm 65:8; 96:12; 98:8; Isaiah 14:7).

When God created man, He intended for him to share this joy—to know deep and abiding pleasure. As Charles Spurgeon says, God made "men capable of happiness; they are in their right element when they are happy."[4]

To that end, God designed the Garden of Eden to be a place of delight for created mankind. And though sin ravaged God's masterpiece like dirty water thrown against the canvas of a Van Gogh, the prophet Isaiah foretold a day when God would restore the earth, making it like Eden—a place of joy and gladness, thanksgiving and song (Isaiah 51:3).

God did not make man for duty or drudgery or even ordinariness. He created Him for joy. This premise has the power to open our eyes to an entire new paradigm of living. It can change how we think about things and how we approach God. Joy is the birthright of every believer, and everything changes when this reality takes root within us.

God Is the Source and Object of Our Joy

I've got the joy, joy, joy, joy
down in my heart.
Where? Down in my heart.
Where? Down in my heart.
I've got the joy, joy, joy, joy
down in my heart.
Where? Down in my heart to stay!

This Sunday school favorite speaks a profound and timeless truth: The presence of God within our souls is the source of our deepest joy. In His final hours, Jesus told the disciples that He was the Vine from whom they could draw all the sustenance for life that they would ever need. By abiding in Him, they would not only experience His joy but also be replete, overflowing with joy—like one of their nets stretched beyond its capacity from an abundance of flopping fish (John 15:11; 16:24).

John Piper calls this Christian hedonism, a term that stunned some and offended others when he first wrote *Desiring God*, a book that is becoming a Christian classic. He explains: "Behind the repentance that turns away from sin and behind the faith that embraces Christ is the birth of a new taste, a new longing, a new passion for the pleasure of God's presence. This is the root of conversion. This is the creation of a Christian hedonist."[5]

God's manifest presence within and without is the wellspring of joy we continually drink from. "In His presence is fullness of joy" (Psalm 16:11). In the Old Testament, the Ark of the Covenant—and later the temple where it was placed—represented the presence of God. When the ark was taken or the temple destroyed, God's people grieved, and when it was returned or restored, they threw a big party.

For example, when retrieving the ark after the Philistines had returned it, David called for a musical parade to accompany him. They entered Jerusalem carrying it on poles; the people shouting; instruments playing; and David leaping, dancing, and celebrating in the streets (1 Chronicles 15).

When Hezekiah reopened the temple after King Ahaz had let it go to ruins, he sent an invitation to all the tribes to come for worship. They celebrated the Passover with joy for seven days and, having such a great time, extended it another seven days. Scripture says there was great joy in Jerusalem because they'd seen nothing like this since the days of King Solomon (2 Chronicles 30:26).

God's presence as represented by His temple filled the people with joy. In the same way, the reality that we are the temple of the living God should strike such a chord within us that we cannot restrain ourselves.

JOY

*Joy is our jubilant response to the presence of the living God
who has made His home within our souls.*

Not only is God the source of our joy but He is also the object. We direct our joy toward Him. Why? Because His Being warrants it. Everything about Him and everything He does is reason for joy, a fact Scripture affirms over and over by commanding us to rejoice. Here are a few examples: He reigns, He saves, and He restores. He sees affliction and He has compassion. He judges, revives, and gives His Word. He brings us into His chambers and loves us, and He does great things (1 Chronicles 16:31; Psalm 13:5; 14:7; 31:7; 48:11; 85:6; 119:162; Song of Solomon 1:4).

When we see who He is and what He has done, we can only rejoice, offering Him the praise due His name. Praise for other people, things, achievements, possessions, life circumstances, or truths takes a distant second in light of knowing God, who by necessity is the object of true joy.

Suffering Expands Our Capacity for Joy

One of the most profound paradoxes of the Christian faith is that what brings the keenest pain in life can also create in us a greater capacity to experience joy. While volumes have been written on the subject, one reason for this is quite simple. The less we have of ourselves, the more room we have for God to manifest himself. Pain diminishes our resources, bringing us to a place of desperate neediness—a place where God himself can come and fill us.

If God is the source of our joy, then it makes sense that experiencing more of Him will increase our joy. Isaiah wrote that when God restored His people, the afflicted would increase their gladness *in the Lord* and the needy of mankind would rejoice *in the Holy One of Israel* (Isaiah 29:19).

Recently I was at a church where the youth pastor had just resigned. One of the younger teenage boys was devastated. Having been abandoned by his own father just a few months before, the youth pastor's departure revisited old wounds and opened up new ones. As I saw the anguish in the boy's eyes, I found myself thinking that no child should have to endure such pain. Immediately the Spirit spoke to my heart and I cried out in silent prayer, *Oh, Lord, let him learn now that You will fill the empty places, that You can come and make up what is lacking . . . that You long to be the joy of his life, the One who will never leave.*

In one of David's darkest moments, as he fled into the wilderness of Judah, he wrote, "My soul is satisfied as with marrow and fatness, and my mouth offers praises with joyful lips. When I remember you on my bed, I meditate on you in the night watches, for you have been my help, and in the shadow of your wings I sing for joy" (Psalm 63:5–7).

Jesus told his disciples that they would experience great suffering when He died, but like a woman in labor, they would forget the anguish when He came to them again, being filled with a joy no one could take away (John 16:19–22). The author of Hebrews tells us that Jesus' ability to endure the cross hinged on the joy that was set before Him. While this joy perhaps reflected a variety of things, surely one was the imminent prospect of reveling once again in the fullness of the Godhead or, in other words, experiencing all of His unified Being (Hebrews 12:1–8).

The enhancement of joy through adversity is a mystery unique to the Christian faith and one we will never fully understand. But Scripture is replete with the message that weeping may last for a night, but joy will surely come in the morning (Psalm 30:5).

Barriers to Joy

In the sunset of his life, Martin Lloyd-Jones, the great British reformed theologian and revivalist, preached of the need for an outpouring of power, indeed for the church to receive a fresh baptism with the Holy Spirit. Whether we agree with his theology or not, we can't help but relate to his sense of urgency concerning the state of the church. He grieved that though he'd spent a lifetime promoting orthodoxy, most reformed churches did not reflect the vibrant life of Christ but instead a kind of monotonous aridity. In his book *Joy Unspeakable*, he wrote, "The Christian is not meant to be a man who is just managing to hold on and who is miserable and unhappy and forcing himself to do these things, dragging himself, as it were, to the house of God."[6]

Why are some just managing to hold on? Why are some Christians miserable and unhappy, having to coerce each other into some form of obedience? What keeps believers from rejoicing in the reality of what they've received? Why is the church of Jesus Christ known more for the stands it takes than the abundant life it embraces? There are many reasons—let us look closely at a few.

We Don't Believe Joy Is Our Birthright

Many Christians today are in a quandary. We cannot deny that a strong desire for pleasure resonates within us. Once we gratified it in fleshly ways— food, drink, sex, achievement, success, fun, sports—any number of things. As we gave our lives to Christ, we fully expected worldly delights to lose their appeal.

What we may not admit, however, is that the yearning for happiness, enjoyment, and pleasure isn't going away like we thought it would. Finding ourselves secretly enticed by the lusts of this world, we don't quite know what to do. Most of us tend to travel down one of three different, but equally destructive, paths.

One group grits their teeth, determined to do the right thing. Suppressing their desire for pleasure, they seek to satisfy their souls with religious activity and spiritual zeal. These may be the hardest workers in the kingdom of God, but the look on their faces or quiet despair within their hearts belies the Good News they claim to live by.

The second group cites a "God loves me the way I am" mantra, claiming that grace sanctions the dangling of their feet in the river of worldly delights. The third group gives up all together, their faith fading into oblivion as they go through the motions of a life with little hope.

All three have missed the mark. God created us with a drive for pleasure so strong that He alone can satisfy it. Jonathan Edwards wrote that because man's mental capacity is so vast, the limited pleasures of this world can never bring him happiness. This is why sin so quickly loses its luster—it is inadequate in its ability to appease our yearnings. No earthly pleasure can ever permeate the depths of a soul created for eternity.

Our true desire for pleasure comes from God and is meant to terminate in God—nothing else will do. Edwards wrote:

> The carnal soul imagines that earthly things are excellent . . . it soon finds an end to their excellency. . . . But Jesus Christ has true excellency, and so great excellency that when they come to see it they look no further, but the mind rests there. It sees a transcendent glory and ineffable sweetness in him; it sees that till now it has been pursuing shadows, but that now it has found the substance; that before it had been seeking happiness in the stream, but that now it has found the ocean.[7]

What a different people we would be if we stopped trying to suppress our longings or justify our lusts, and instead ran after an infinite God to meet our endless cravings for joy.

We Waste Our Sorrows

Though God intends suffering to expand our capacity for joy, many experience the opposite, becoming embittered and hardened in the face of struggle. What makes the difference? Psalm 126:6 may provide a clue: "He who goes to and fro weeping, carrying his bag of seed, shall indeed come again with a shout of joy, bringing his sheaves with him." The condition for joy is the sowing of seed. What does this mean?

When the Israelites returned from captivity in Babylon, the ground they had once farmed was desolate and barren. Overgrown weeds and sharp rocks threatened them with every step. Sowing seed was a painful process—they had to clear the debris, dig up thorny weeds, and cast out rough stones. Only then could the seed take root in order to yield a precious harvest for their hungry families.

The human heart is much the same. To enjoy the fruit of greater joy, we have to diligently work the soil of our souls. This doesn't happen automatically. Many people waste their sorrows, feeling the pain but never reaping the reward of a deeper experience of God's presence.

Paul says in Romans 5:1–5 that we can rejoice in our trials, for they produce perseverance leading to proven character, and that proven character produces hope. The word "hope" here means "to anticipate with pleasure." Paul assures us that when we have hope, we will not be disappointed. Why? Because in tribulation, the love of God is poured out—completely expended—within our hearts (v. 5). Through the trials we face, we can anticipate with pleasure a more profound encounter with our divine Lover.

One day, soon after their return to Jerusalem, some Israelites reminisced together over their painful past while exiled in Babylon. One spoke of the day they sat by a river, having hung their harps on the willow tree nearby. Some of their captors, noticing the instruments, had begun to taunt them, goading them to sing a song of joy—the kind they used to sing before they were ravaged by the Chaldeans. One Israelite cried out this poignant plea: "How can we sing the Lord's song in a foreign land?" (Psalm 137:4).

Indeed. This is the question we wrestle with when sorrow approaches and we have no song to sing. Saint Therese of Lisieux, known as the "little flower," sought to answer this in a letter to her sister:

How then, shall we be able to sing the Lord's canticles in a strange land? Our God, the Guest of our soul . . . comes to us with the intention of finding an abode, an empty tent, in the midst of the earth's field of battle. He asks only this, and He Himself is the Divine Musician who takes charge of the concert. . . . Ah! If only we were to hear this ineffable harmony, if one single vibration were to reach our ears![8]

The master Musician tunes the strings of our broken hearts, and we feel the stabs of pain at every turn of the key. But when He is done, He plays a song we could never have heard amid the humdrum of a carefree existence. It is a song of joy—every note a sweet aroma designed to soothe the anguish of our soul.

We Devalue the Love of God

Twenty-five years ago, on a warm spring night, I opened my heart to the guy I'm now married to. We'd pursued a wonderful friendship for almost two years, but something happened to me along the way—I fell in love. For a while I had said nothing, but finally I could hold it in no longer. Mustering up my courage, I muttered something about why the relationship couldn't go on as it had and blurted out, "I love you."

The suffocating silence that followed was almost unbearable. At last he answered with words I've never forgotten: "Well, all I can say is that this doesn't bother me."

Oddly enough, the guy was trying to encourage me. He thought that since most of his friends were afraid of love and marriage, the fact that my newly proclaimed ardor didn't scare him off was a positive thing—something that should make me feel okay about the risk I'd taken in sharing.

Instead, I was devastated. I wanted bells and whistles, a jig or a hoot and holler but instead got a shrug. Needless to say, his heart changed in the coming months, but for a while I lived with the pain of unrequited love.

The memory of that night came back to me recently as I pondered the love of God. I saw Him standing at the wall of the worlds whispering, *I love you. I love you. I love you.* And I shrugged, going on as if the most mind-boggling thing in the universe had not just occurred. What hurt our eternal Lover endures and how we devalue the love He pours out on us through our nonchalance.

We shrug when we sing songs of worship without deep swells of emotion bubbling up inside of us. We shrug when we take action to solve our own problems, doubting that God cares enough to come through. We shrug when we are cavalier about His Word, acting as if we've mastered its truths. We shrug when we ignore the two billion people in this world who've never even heard Christ's name. We shrug when we live for our own agenda, our success, our plans. We shrug every time we wake up in the morning and do not cry out to His exalted presence, full of gratitude for another day of life.

The love of God for sinners is a preposterous thing. Even as I try to write of it, I am overwhelmed. That the Creator of the cosmos, holy Adonai, omnipotent El Shaddai, the great I AM, who has always been and forever will be, deigns to love me is unimaginable, almost unspeakable.

And how were the angels compelled to share the incredible news that the Son of the most high God had come to bring His love to mankind? "Behold, I bring you good news of *great joy*, which will be for all the people" (Luke 2:10). God's love is the good news—and if it doesn't fill our hearts with joy, we've never seen it. We may have memorized John 3:16, but if we can say it and shrug, we've missed the whole point.

God's love is as grandiose as He is—it is fiery, consuming, passionate, all-absorbing, even suffocating—for He will not let go, ever. We can't corral God's love or even make sense of it. We can't contain it or downsize its effects. He loves us. He goes to His death for love of us and daily faces the heartache of those who keep a disinterested distance, depreciating the price He paid to make them His own.

One of Jesus' final prayers speaks of this love, revealing something so utterly unthinkable that if we understood it, we'd never get over the joy of it. "Just as the Father has loved Me, I have also loved you; abide in My love" (John 15:9). Consider—the love that exists among the members of the triune Godhead is extended to you and to me—we are given the amazing privilege of living in that reality. And when we do, we will experience abounding, overflowing joy. "These things I have spoken to you so that My joy may be in you, and that your joy may be made full" (John 15:11).

Paul lived out this truth. He prayed that we would be rooted and grounded in God's love—that we would know its length and height and depth and breadth, even though it was beyond comprehension. Then he says the most incredible thing—that to know this love is to be "filled with all the fullness of God" (Ephesians 3:13–19). We should be struck dumb at such a statement, but instead we shrug. We've become a "people who say they believe in Jesus but who are no longer astonished and amazed."[9]

When we come to know *and* believe the love that God has for us (1 John 4:16), our lives can never be mediocre again. Tears will flow freely in His presence, our hearts will flutter at the thought of Him, our feet will be set to dancing, and yes, hoots and hollers of joy will escape our lips.

What We Must Do

Today I feel great sadness for those who have not yet found their way out of the labyrinth of legalism I grew up in. I see there a mass of lifeless bodies, weary from the duty of religion. Vast numbers have dropped out, and many who continue to populate sanctuaries on Sundays are still trying to assuage their guilt for no longer being able to maintain fidelity to a creed that has left them dry and barren.

As Brennan Manning says in his book *The Ragamuffin Gospel*, something is radically wrong. In describing the inevitable outcome of a joyless gospel, he writes:

There begins a long winter of discontent that eventually flowers into gloom, pessimism, and subtle despair: subtle because it goes un-recognized, unnoticed, and therefore unchallenged. It takes the form of boredom, drudgery. We are overcome by the ordinariness of life, by daily duties done over and over again. We secretly admit that the call of Jesus is too demanding, that surrender to the Spirit is beyond our reach. We start acting like everyone else. Life takes on a joyless, empty quality. . . . Something is radically wrong.[10]

Perhaps you have walked that road . . . perhaps you are on it even now. What must we do to break out of our "winter of discontent"? How can we learn to live in the tremendous joy of the Good News? First, we have to see with spiritual eyes—to really grab hold of—what the Good News means. Then we must learn the secret of abiding in God's love and walking in the power of His Holy Spirit.

Rely on Divine Revelation

Lately one thought dominates my spiritual thinking: *All I know is I don't know very much.* I suppose this is a good thing, for I am finally at peace with my inadequacy and have come to understand how desperately I need God to reveal truth to me.

One of the greatest needs in the body of Christ today is spiritual reve-lation. We've methodically established our doctrine, made a science of study-ing Scripture, dissected prayer into every possible combination of compo-nents, and can cite principles of church growth backward and forward. But the joy of childlike faith eludes us.

In Jesus' priestly prayer the night before He died, He revealed the raw truth of what He was about. "Father, I desire that they also, whom You have given Me, be with Me where I am, so that they may see My glory" (John 17:24). The essence of the Good News is that the Son of God desired a people who would be with Him, so that He could show them His glory. "That they . . . [would] be with me, where I am."

When the eyes of our heart are opened up to this, joy floods our souls—

everlasting joy. Like the merchant in Jesus' parable, we will sell everything to gain this one precious pearl. Unfortunately, we haven't grasped it, and instead we haggle with God about giving percentages, ministry priorities, or thirty-minute quiet times. Tired of serving, we admit our complacency but aren't appalled at our limpid lives.

We desperately need spiritual illumination, for how in the world can we ever hope to unravel the mystery of a God who gives himself to man? We can't. But God can—His Spirit within us searches the very depths of God, "so that we may know the things freely given to us by God" (1 Corinthians 2:10–12).

If the idea that Jesus wants you to be with Him for now and eternity doesn't stir something deep in the core of your soul, it is time that you take stock of your religiosity. Rely no more on truths you've gleaned, studied, memorized, analyzed, and accumulated, and instead simply cry out to God. The only thing and the best thing you can do is plead with His Spirit to reveal to you the "true knowledge of God's mystery, that is, *Christ Himself*, in whom are hidden all the treasures of wisdom and knowledge" (Colossians 2:2–3).

Cry out, and don't stop crying out until the joy of the Lord floods your entire being. And when it does, cry out some more, for the depths of delight in the river of God are inexhaustible.

Abide in God's Love

On some days, in the quiet stillness of the morning after everyone has left for work or school, I close the blinds, put on some worship music, and . . . dance before the Lord. I'm not much of a hoofer—I don't have any jazz or ballet moves with which to dazzle God. As I begin, I feel shy and a little tentative. But soon, caught up in the rapture of redeeming love, my feeble offering becomes a work of art for the master Choreographer. And when this happens—wonder of wonders—I feel God's pleasure.

The abiding joy of the Christian life comes as we learn to delight in

God's love and receive His delight in us. This was the plan that mankind's sin derailed. Throughout Scripture, God offers hints of what this once looked like and what His people will again experience. Isaiah wrote:

> For behold, I create new heavens and a new earth; and the former things will not be remembered or come to mind. But be glad and rejoice forever in what I create; for behold, I create Jerusalem for rejoicing and her people for gladness. I will also rejoice in Jerusalem and be glad in My people; and there will no longer be heard in her the voice of weeping and the sound of crying. (Isaiah 65:17–19)

The cycle of joy God speaks of is an amazing thing. We, God's people, are made for gladness. Beholding the wonder of this world—the hue of a golden sunset or the sound of a singing sparrow or the love of our family—we can't help but rejoice. Something wells up in us when we consider that we are *fearfully and wonderfully made*. We ponder the grandeur of *agape* and are overcome with awe. We cannot be silent or unmoved in the face of such things.

Singing or shouting or leaping or dancing, our praise ascends like incense to this One who made us, who loves us ferociously. Then He takes pleasure in our experience of Him. In fact, He exults over us with joy and rejoices over us with shouts of joy! The voice of the Bridegroom for His bride is one of gladness (Zephaniah 3:17; Jeremiah 33:11).

I have not always been able to appreciate the depths of God's love, for I could not really believe He delighted in me. But one day at the end of a long period of crying out, I collapsed like a child into His arms, learning for the first time the incredible peace of lying immobile against His breast. Like the old hymn, I could finally sing: "Jesus, I am resting, resting, in the joy of what Thou art." As I reflect on my journey to that point, I understand now why I struggled to let Him love me—to abide in His love.

The trap of duty-driven faith had bound me. Confusing God's love with His approval, I ever lived to maintain the status I thought I'd earned through diligent obedience. Thus I could not delight in Him because I made Him small in my eyes—attainable and manageable—a God whose expectations I would live up to or die trying.

How absurd. When we try to harness God's love to a wagonload of works, we make light of His infinite nature. It is no trifling matter to be the object of God's love. He is, as Jonathan Edwards wrote:

> ... the Creator of the World, and by whom all things consist, and who is exalted at God's right hand, and made head over principalities and powers in heavenly places, who has all things put under his feet, and is King of Kings and Lord of Lords, and is the brightness of the Father's glory! Surely to be beloved by him, is enough to satisfy the soul of a worm of the dust.[11]

Abiding in God's love is not about what we do but about who He is and what He has already done. This is where we lack faith. We struggle to believe in the Good Shepherd who found us lost and alone and carried us on His shoulders dancing and leaping into the fold, while myriad angels threw a party in our behalf (Luke 15:3–7). Julian of Norwich, a sixteenth-century believer, said, "Some of us believe that God is almighty and can do everything; and that he is all-wise and may do everything; but that he is all-love and will do everything—there we draw back. As I see it, this ignorance is the greatest of all hindrances to God's lovers."[12]

It is a great hindrance indeed. Jesus made an audacious statement when He proclaimed that He loves us in the same way the Father loves Him. Consider this once again—are you beginning to fathom it at all? That the love shared within the Godhead is extended to you? He calls us to abide in this—to make our home in it, to dwell within the boundaries of His boundless love. In this our joy is made full, for we love Him, rejoicing with *joy inexpressible and full of glory* (John 15:9–11).

Walk in the Spirit

Joy is a manifestation of the Holy Spirit within us. The early church was characterized as a people continually filled with joy and with the Holy Spirit. If we are filled with the Holy Spirit, joy will bubble out of us in "psalms and hymns and spiritual songs, singing and making melody with our hearts to the Lord always giving thanks for all things" (Ephesians 5:19–20).

When we depend on our own strength to live the Christian life, we immediately lose the joy of the Spirit within us, for we are walking according to the flesh. Paul said that these two things simply could not coexist. "For the flesh sets its desire against the Spirit, and the Spirit against the flesh; for these are in opposition to one another, so that you may not do the things that you please" (Galatians 5:17).

In the end, we don't even accomplish the works we set out to do—it is impossible to please God under such circumstances (Romans 8:8). When the Pharisees challenged Jesus for breaking the rules of faith they so self-righteously adhered to, He gave them two word pictures to describe the absurdity of man depending on his own works.

First, He said it was like tearing a piece of cloth from a new garment to patch up an old tattered one. Both garments are ruined in the process. Next, he likened it to putting new wine into an old wineskin that bursts open. It simply can't be done. Then He adds a profound statement: "And no one, after drinking old wine wishes for new; for he says, 'The old is good enough' " (Luke 5:36–39).

When I saw what this verse was really saying, I began to understand one of the tragedies of the church today—the great dearth of middle-aged, mature, joyful believers. More and more when I speak across the country, spiritually hungry young men and women approach me to discuss their walk with God. Inevitably they long for mentors to help them mature in Christ. There just aren't enough wise saints to meet the spiritual needs of those God is saving and bringing into the kingdom.

So often I hear older believers say things like: "I did my work and I'm tired; I'm going to rest now." And I wonder what ever motivated them in the first place. If it was God himself, then what happened? Surely He hasn't changed. Jesus seems to be saying in this passage that as they drank from the old wine of duty-driven service, they ceased to desire the new wine of His Spirit.

Walking in the flesh, depending on what we do for God to produce spiritual fruit, not only casts aspersion on His Holy Spirit but actually diminishes our desire for Him. What a frightful destiny—one that guarantees a life void of joy, for it is a life void of the manifest presence of God. If we want to experience the joy of the Spirit-filled life, let us not "contaminate His glory with our sweat."[13]

Joy Changes Everything

In 1623 a woman in France gave birth to one of the greatest mathematical minds this world has ever known. From early on he demonstrated amazing genius, discovering quite by himself, at the age of twelve, that the sum of the angles of a triangle is equal to two right angles—a fact now taught in every basic geometry class. His name was Blaise Pascal, and he spent his life conducting mathematical experiments and giving lectures. One night he had an experience that changed everything.

At the age of thirty-one, he was driving a coach home when the lead horses took fright and fled wildly across a bridge railing into the dark waters below. Had the reins not snapped, Pascal would have plunged to his death, a reality that stunned him. Later that night he experienced the presence of God in a dramatic way. He wrote of it on a piece of parchment, secured it in an amulet, and kept it next to his heart for the rest of his life.

From that time forth, Pascal gave up his mathematical pursuits and devoted himself to Christ. Upon his death they found the paper containing these words:

This day of Grace 1654;
From about half past ten at night to
about half after midnight,
Fire.
God of Abraham, God of Isaac, God of Jacob,
not of the philosophers and the wise.
Security, security. Feeling, joy, peace.
God of Jesus Christ,
Thy God shall be my God.
Forgetfulness of the world and of all save God. . . .
O righteous Father, the world hath not known Thee,
but I have known Thee.
Joy, joy, joy, tears of joy. . . .[14]

Blaise Pascal encountered God and was never the same. Joy so filled his life that he could not go back to the life he'd known, though it held all the glamour of worldly success and esteem. He was intoxicated by God, held in His embrace, and astounded by His ways. In his classic work *Pensées* (Thoughts), Pascal wrote a philosophical treatise worthy of the incredible mind he possessed. But often from the pages rings the simple truth of God's love and the joy it brought him:

> But the God of Abraham, the God of Isaac, the God of Jacob, the God of Christians, is a God of love and of comfort, a God who fills the soul and heart of those whom He possesses, a God who makes them conscious of their inward wretchedness, and His infinite mercy, who unites Himself to their inmost soul, who fills it with humility and joy, with confidence and love, who renders them incapable of any other end than Himself.[15]

Pascal grasped that God had made us for himself and that no other end would ever satisfy. Truly, the joy of the crucified life terminates on the infinite I AM who created us in His image that we might be able to know

Him, to see and embrace His glory, and live in the light of His ineffable Being. He has rendered us incapable of any other end than himself. Herein lies the joy that swallows every sorrow, the happiness that ever outshines the trifling pleasures of a fallen world.

TAKING UP OUR CROSS—
What We Gain and What We Lose

Joy over what God holds out to us should fill our hearts, compelling us to run after Him, sparing no cost. This is God's plan, for He finds no pleasure in duty-driven service. If we serve Him out of obligation, we will soon turn to other things to meet our desire for pleasure. In the end, these things become our enemies, binding and restricting our hearts.

Gain Desire
"The kingdom of heaven is like a treasure hidden in the field, which a man found and hid again; and from joy over it he goes and sells all that he has and buys that field" (Matthew 13:44).

Lose Duty
"Because you did not serve the Lord your God with joy and a glad heart, for the abundance of all things; therefore you shall serve your enemies whom the Lord will send against you ... and He will put an iron yoke on your neck" (Deuteronomy 28:47–48).

The joy of God's presence offers us a fullness of life unparalleled by anything of this world. Often, though, we turn back to weak substitutes, trying to seal our identity with activity and accomplishment. God continually woos us, reminding us that life is about the delight of knowing Him—nothing more and nothing less.

Gain Delight

"They drink their fill of the abundance of your house; and you give them to drink of the river of your delights. For with you is the fountain of life; in your light we see light" (Psalm 36:8–9).

Lose Drudgery

"But now that you have come to know God, or rather to be known by God, how is it that you turn back again to the weak and worthless elemental things, to which you desire to be enslaved all over again?" (Galatians 4:9).

When the struggles of life ensue, our hope comes from knowing that God will never leave or forsake us. His love is our support and gives us the strength to carry on with gladness. A soul who doesn't live in the joy of this hope faces a barren future, void of the sustaining pleasure of God's commitment to him.

Gain Hope

"Now may our Lord Jesus Christ Himself and God our Father, who has loved us and given us eternal comfort and good hope by grace, comfort and strengthen your hearts in every good work and word" (2 Thessalonians 2:16–17).

Lose Barrenness

" 'You look for much, but behold, it comes to little; when you bring it home, I blow it away. Why?' declares the Lord of hosts, 'Because of My house which lies desolate, while each of you runs to his own house. Therefore, because of you the sky has withheld its dew and the earth has withheld its produce' " (Haggai 1:9–10).

The joy of God's presence is far more than an emotion—it is a strengthening factor in all we do, enabling us to persevere with courage toward the goal of eternity with Him. Without it, we are like weak-kneed babes, always tripping over obstacles like guilt, disappointment, sin, and fear.

Gain Strength

"Splendor and majesty are before Him, strength and joy are in His place" (1 Chronicles 16:27).

"Do not be grieved, for the joy of the Lord is your strength" (Nehemiah 8:10).

Lose Stumbling

"Now to Him who is able to keep you from stumbling, and to make you stand in the presence of His glory blameless with great joy" (Jude 1:24).

An old adage states: *Your troubles can make you or they can break you—it's up to you.* As believers we take great comfort in the fact that it really isn't up to us. God meets us in the core of our sorrows, revealing himself, comforting us and carrying us through. Without the joy of His nurturing sustenance, we are subject to melancholy moods that drag us down and sap us of life.

Gain Comfort

"I will rejoice and be glad in your lovingkindness, because you have seen my affliction; you have known the troubles of my soul" (Psalm 31:7).

"They will obtain gladness and joy, and sorrow and sighing will flee away. I, even I, am He who comforts you" (Isaiah 51:11b–12a).

Lose Despondency

"To grant those who mourn in Zion, giving them a garland instead of ashes, the oil of gladness instead of mourning, the mantle of praise instead of a spirit of fainting. So they will be called oaks of righteousness, the plant-

ing of the Lord, that He may be glorified" (Isaiah 61:3).

It is hard to imagine why we would sacrifice joy, settling instead for the drudgery of following rules. Stumbling along, barren and despondent, we are poor testimonies to the God who created us for pleasure. When we take up our cross against these things, we can live with desire for our Lord, enjoying the delight of His presence, being filled with hope and strength, resting always in the comfort of His loving arms. Why would we ever resist?

PRACTICING JOY—
A Mini-Retreat

When the Israelites walked in the light of God's amazing covenant with them, their lives were characterized by joy. They partied often—their religious feasts being a celebration of God's goodness to them. But as they strayed from the relationship with Him, they began to forget the covenant benefits He had for them. Many of the prophets' pleas were based on this premise—they were a cry from the heart of God to delight in Him and His ways. The call to repent was simply an enticement to joy, one that God issues to every one of us this very moment. Let us run after this inestimable treasure.

Preparing Your Heart

God wants to fill us with joy, and when He does, we find ourselves wanting to express it in some way. Thus in seeking Him, we will spend the bulk of our time in thanksgiving and praise, looking for ways to give expression to the joy God plants in our hearts.

Welcome God's presence with you, thanking Him that He is faithful to meet you and manifest himself to you. Offer this time to Him to do with as He wills.

Read the first chapter of Ephesians, which tells some of the things that we have already gained because of Christ's commitment to us. As you read each verse, pause and give thanks out loud to the Lord.

When you have finished, read it again, this time pausing to reflect on what each glorious gift from God means to your life today. Consider what your life would look like if He hadn't called you to this. Ask His Spirit to write these things on your heart.

Write a response in your prayer journal.

Contemplating His Presence

To really know the fulfillment of expressing our joy, we have to resist religious stereotypes that remove emotion from worship. We are an emotional people—God made us that way. And though we may differ in our expressions of worship, the hundreds of commandments to rejoice from Scripture affirm that we must express our joy in some manner.

It is interesting to note that often we find it easier to express ourselves concerning the things of this world than in view of the glory of the living God. For example, we have no problem shouting at a ball game but are uncomfortable raising our voice in praise, though God commands us to. For a moment, imagine yourself in a couple of the following scenarios. Try to picture how you would physically respond to each one:

- The Prize Patrol shows up at your door with a check for one million dollars.
- Your son, after years of labor in Little League, has been drafted to the pros and you are in the stands at his first game.
- Your boss has offered you the position you've dreamed of for years and you are on your way home to tell your family.
- You've just come in from your twelfth date with a wonderful guy (or girl) and it is just becoming clear that you are in love.
- Your high school basketball team won the state championship and you made the winning shot.

- You've always dreamed of being parents and you just got the test results that you are going to be!

As you picture yourself in some of these situations, what kinds of expressions do you give for the joy you feel? (Do you jump up and down, shout, call everyone you know, whistle, sing?)

Now consider the unlimited and eternal benefits you have in Christ. How do you express your profound joy? Does the reality of your relationship with Him well up within you until you must find a way to express it? Remember that joy in Scripture is usually characterized by some kind of response—most often singing, dancing, weeping, or shouting in worship and thanksgiving.

Ask the Holy Spirit to rain on you, immersing you in His joy. Read Ephesians 2:1–3 out loud, focusing on what has been done for you. Wait on the Holy Spirit to reveal truth. Read the verses again, crying out to Him for spiritual insight.

In what ways might you express your joy at such amazing things? Consider the possibilities listed below and choose one, or come up with your own. Then take the time to express uninhibited joy before the Lord in worship for the things you have seen.

Some possible expressions are:

- Put on a worship CD and sing along with heartfelt worship.
- Go for a run, experiencing the grace of God in every step, thanking and praising Him aloud as you go.
- Find a place where you won't be distracted or be a distraction to others, and read a Psalm of praise at the top of your lungs—shouting for joy.
- Write a poem or prose expressing your joy and read it aloud to the audience of One.
- Play some worship music and dance before the Lord, delighting in His joy over you.
- If you play a musical instrument, spend an extended time playing just to

express your joy and experience God's love.

- Choose a passage from one of the prophets that tells of God's heart for His people (Isaiah 43, 44, or others), and read it with dramatic expression, letting God fill you with a sense of the Word's power.

There are many ways to express joy, and you will have others that are meaningful to you. Know that at first you may feel inhibited, but often our struggle is because of the influence of our culture or bad religious experiences from our past. Nevertheless, joy in Scripture carries the connotation of "spinning around with pleasure." If we experience joy, then there must be expression, and in the expression we will find our joy actually increasing.

Responding to His Call

The greatest response of joy is a life that follows Jesus Christ. Physical expression, no matter how heartfelt, does not mean anything to God if joy doesn't make us want to give Him every part of our lives.

Spend some time in a prayer of commitment. Ask God what He wants to do in and through you and what action you might need to take to be completely available to Him.

End your time reading Psalm 96 as praise to God.

Going Forward

The journey of the crucified life is truly beyond our wildest dreams. God delights in our desire for Him and ever lives to woo us to himself. There is nothing worth keeping once we see Him standing there, arms extended. In writing this book, I have felt continually inadequate to even begin to reveal the pleasures of knowing Christ, my Lord. My deep and heartfelt prayer is that you will see something—even one thing—that will so grab your attention that you can never go back to the ordinary again. God's promises are extravagant and His commitment to you secure. Live in the wonder of what He has done. And may every moment of your brief time left on this earth be filled with passion to embrace the gain of the crucified life.

Notes

1. Patricia Klein, Evelyn Bence, Jane Campbell, Laura Pearson, and David Wimbish, *Growing Up Born Again: A Whimsical Look at the Blessings and Tribulations of Growing Up Born Again* (Old Tappan, N.J.: Fleming H. Revell, 1987), 52.
2. *Vine's Expository Dictionary of Biblical Words.*
3. *Strong's* definition.
4. Charles Haddon Spurgeon, "Christ's Joy and Ours," from *Spurgeon's Expository Encyclopedia: Sermons by Charles H. Spurgeon* (Grand Rapids: Baker Books, reprint, 1996).
5. John Piper, *Desiring God: Meditations of a Christian Hedonist* (Portland, Ore.: Multnomah Press, 1996), 69–70.
6. Lloyd-Jones, 102.
7. Jonathan Edwards, *Jonathan Edwards on Knowing Christ* (Carlisle, Pa.: The Banner of Truth Trust, 1997), 169–70.
8. St. Therese of Lisieux, trans., John Clark, *Letters of St. Therese of Lisieux*, volume 2 (Washington: Washington Province of Discalced Carmelites, Inc., 1988), 863.
9. Michael Yaconelli, *Dangerous Wonder* (Colorado Springs: NavPress, 1998), 24.
10. Manning, 17.
11. Edwards, 171.
12. Julian of Norwich, *The Revelations of Divine Love* (New York: Penguin Books, 1966), 56.
13. Roxanne Brant, *Ministering to the Lord* (Springdale, Pa.: Whitaker House, 1993), 57.
14. As quoted by Martin Lloyd-Jones in *Joy Unspeakable*, 107.
15. Blaise Pascal, *Pensées* (public domain).

FURTHER RECOMMENDED READING

The Sacred Romance: Drawing Closer to the Heart of God, Brent Curtis & John Eldredge (Thomas Nelson Publishers, 1997).

The Hour That Changes the World, Dick Eastman (Fleming H. Revell, 1990).

The End for Which God Created the World, Jonathan Edwards, edited and annotated by John Piper.

Jonathan Edwards on Knowing Christ, Jonathan Edwards (Banner of Truth Trust, 1997).

Celebration of Discipline, Richard Foster (Harper & Row, 1978).

Prayer: Finding the Heart's True Home, Richard Foster (Harper San Francisco, 1992).

Abba's Child, Brennan Manning (NavPress, 1994).

The Ragamuffin Gospel, Brennan Manning (Multnomah Press, 1990).

Mind on Fire, an updated and rearranged version of *Pensées*, Blaise Pascal, edited and updated by James Houston (Bethany House Publishers, 1998).

Desiring God: Meditations of a Christian Hedonist, tenth-anniversary expanded edition, John Piper (Multnomah Press, 1996).

Future Grace: The Purifying Power of Living by Faith, John Piper (Multnomah Press, 1996).

God's Passion for His Glory, John Piper. An exposition on Jonathan Edwards' book *The End for Which God Created the World* (Crossway Books, 1998).

The Pleasures of God: Meditations on God's Delight in Being God, John Piper (Multnomah Press, 1991).

The Knowledge of the Holy, A. W. Tozer (Harper & Row, 1961).

The Pursuit of God, A. W. Tozer (Harper & Row, n.d.). Subsequent edition available from Christian Publications, 1993.